How

MW01181096

Basic Principles for Studying God's Word

The Bible Teacher's Guide

Gregory Brown

Publishing

2

Endorsements

"The Bible Teacher's Guide … will help any teacher study and get a better background for his/her Bible lessons. In addition, it will give direction and scope to teaching of the Word of God. Praise God for this contemporary introduction to the Word of God."

—Dr. Elmer Towns
Co-founder of Liberty University
Former Dean, Liberty Baptist Theological Seminary

"Expositional, theological, and candidly practical! I highly recommend The Bible Teacher's Guide for anyone seeking to better understand or teach God's Word."

—Dr. Young–Gil Kim
Founding President, Handong Global University

"Helpful to both the layman and the serious student, The Bible Teacher's Guide, by Dr. Greg Brown, is outstanding!"

—Dr. Neal Weaver
President, Louisiana Baptist University

"Whether you are preparing a Bible study, a sermon, or simply wanting to dive deeper into a personal study of God's Word, these will be very helpful tools."

—Eddie Byun
Associate Professor of Christian Ministry, Biola University
Author of Justice Awakening

"I am happy that Greg is making his insights into God's truth available to a wider audience through these books. They bear the hallmarks of good Bible teaching: the result of rigorous Bible study and thoroughgoing application to the lives of people."

—Ajith Fernando
Teaching Director, Youth for Christ
Author of A Call to Joy and Pain

"The content of the series is rich. My prayer is that God will use it to help the body of Christ grow strong."

—Dr. Min Chung
Senior Pastor, Covenant Fellowship Church, Urbana, Illinois
Adjunct Professor, Urbana Theological Seminary

"Knowing the right questions to ask and how to go about answering them is fundamental to learning in any subject matter. Greg demonstrates this convincingly."

—Dr. William Moulder
Professor of Biblical Studies, Trinity International University

Content

Preface

And entrust what you heard me say in the presence of many others as witnesses to faithful people who will be competent to teach others as well.
2 Timothy 2:2 (NET)

Paul's words to Timothy still apply to us today. The church needs teachers who clearly and fearlessly teach the Word of God. With this in mind, The Bible Teacher's Guide (BTG) series was created. This series includes both expositional and topical studies, with resources to help teachers lead small groups, pastors prepare sermons, and individuals increase their knowledge of God's Word.

How to Study the Bible can be used for personal study or as an eight-session small group curriculum. For small groups, the members will read a chapter and discuss the reflection questions (and anything else that stood out in the reading) within their gathering. The chapter can also be read before the gathering, with the meeting focusing only on discussion.

Introduction

There is quite a bit of confusion over how to study the Bible. This confusion can lead to extremes—including hesitancy in approaching the Bible at all (as though it can never be understood) or, on the other spectrum, heretical doctrine. God has given us his Word to be read, studied, understood, enjoyed, applied, and shared. It is meant to be one of our greatest joys, for within Scripture we hear God's voice and understand his will for our lives and others. Consider what David proclaimed about Scripture, "O how I love your law! All day long I meditate on it...Your words are sweeter in my mouth than honey!" (Psalm 119:97, 103). Likewise, Job declared, "I have treasured the words of his mouth more than my daily bread" (Job 23:12b NIV). In *How to Study the Bible*, we learn the great benefits of studying Scripture, hindrances to study, necessary skills and tools, and various Bible study methods, among other things. May God richly deepen your love, appreciation, and understanding of one of his greatest gifts to us, his written Word!

Reasons to Study Scripture

Unfortunately, many Christians struggle with establishing and practicing a plan for reading and studying the Bible. Why? For many reasons. One of them is a lack of motivation. As with any endeavor, if we don't recognize how beneficial something is, we will struggle with motivation and without motivation, we won't do it, or won't do it consistently.

This is, in part, why Scripture repeatedly teaches about the benefits of studying the Word of God. It challenges us to study, not only because God calls us to do so, but also because there are so many blessings for us when we do. In this lesson, we will consider ten reasons for studying Scripture, with the goal of becoming motivated to study God's Word with greater dedication and continuity.

People Should Study Scripture to Learn About Salvation—How to Have Eternal Life

In 2 Timothy 3:15, Paul told Timothy to continue in what he had learned—referring to the Scriptures—because it was able to give him "wisdom for salvation through faith in Christ Jesus." Scripture gives people wisdom on how to be saved. The Old Testament tells the story of God creating the earth, the world falling into sin and disarray, and God's promise to redeem the world through a male child. It reveals that the child would have a Jewish lineage and that the child would be both human and divine. Then,

14

the Gospels reveal this person as Jesus, the Son of God. The Son of God lived, died on the cross for our sins, and rose from the dead, so we could have eternal life through faith in him. People should read the Bible because no other book teaches about how a person can be saved. The Bible teaches redemptive history—how God saves the world.

People Should Study Scripture to Grow in Righteousness

In 2 Timothy 3:16-17, Paul said, "All Scripture is God-breathed and is useful for teaching, rebuking, correcting and training in righteousness, so that the man of God may be thoroughly equipped for every good work." After people accept Christ, Scripture gives them "teaching" or "doctrine." This is one of the elements that makes Christianity unique in comparison to other religions. It is filled with doctrine. Scripture not only teaches the doctrine of salvation but also the doctrine of God. God is a triune God: a trinity. He is God the Father, God the Son, and God the Holy Spirit. They are three independent persons, co-equal, and yet one.

The Bible teaches the doctrine of humanity (or anthropology). People were made in the image of God and reflect God in various ways, including through being male and female (cf. Gen 1:27, 1 Cor 11:3). It teaches the doctrine of the Holy Spirit. The Holy Spirit is the third person of the Trinity. God gave the Holy Spirit to convict unbelievers and lead them to the truth; additionally, the Holy Spirit is given to believers to empower them and transform them into the image of God. The Bible is filled with doctrinal teachings, which we need for life and godliness.

In addition, the Bible rebukes us by revealing the ways we are in sin and calls us to repent. The Bible also corrects us by not only showing us how we are wrong, but how to get right. Finally, the Bible trains us for every good work, which includes being a godly spouse, parent, child, worker, or leader. This is what we call

15

the sufficiency of Scripture: it equips us for every good work. The more a person knows God's Word, the more God can use them to bless others.

People Should Study Scripture to Discern God's Direction

In Psalm 119:105, David said, "Your word is a lamp to walk by, and a light to illumine my path." For David, to be in the Word was to be able to see clearly and make decisions about going to the left or to the right. To not be in the Word was to make decisions in the dark. The Bible tells us what to do in moral situations—do not lie, steal, or cheat—and also gives us principles for all situations, including marriage, parenting, work, and conflict, to name just a few examples. Proverbs 11:14 says there is victory or safety in the multitude of counselors. We should seek wisdom from other godly people in making decisions. Romans 12:2 teaches us about how to better discern God's direction. It says, "Do not be conformed to this present world, but be transformed by the renewing of your mind, so that you may test and approve what is the will of God—what is good and well-pleasing and perfect." Many can't discern God's voice because the world's voice is so strong in their ears. The more we reject sin and the teachings of the world, and instead renew our minds according to God's Word, the more we'll be able to better discern God's clear guidance.

People Should Study Scripture to Have a Fruitful Life

Psalm 1:1-3 (NIV) says:

Blessed is the one who does not walk in step with the wicked or stand in the way that sinners take or sit in the company of mockers, but whose delight is in the law of the

16

LORD, and who meditates on his law day and night. That person is like a tree planted by streams of water, which yields its fruit in season and whose leaf does not wither—whatever they do prospers.

David described how a person who rejects the world and sin and instead delights and meditates on God's Word will become like a tree. What does the tree metaphor signify? Trees are not made for their own pleasure but for the pleasure and security of others. God said to Abraham, "I will bless you and you will be a blessing" (Gen 12:1-3). People would eat from the fruit of Abraham's life (and his descendants) and find nourishment. Similarly, God will use those who delight in and live in Scripture to bless many. In fact, the Psalmist says, "whatever they do prospers" (v. 3).

Unlike the fruitful person in Psalm 1 whose life is a blessing to others, many people are consumed with themselves. They are takers instead of givers. That is the natural disposition of people apart from God; however, when we allow God to rule in our lives—specifically through living in and obeying his Word—he makes us givers. We become like trees, bearing fruit that many will eat.

People Should Study Scripture to Conquer Sin and Temptations from the Devil

In Psalm 119:11 (NIV), David said, "I have hidden your word in my heart that I might not sin against you." By hiding Scripture in his heart, David was able to defeat sin. This is exactly what Christ did when tempted in the wilderness by Satan: He defeated Satan by quoting Scripture (Matt 4). Similarly, 1 John 2:14 says, "I have written to you, young people, that you are strong, and the word of God resides in you, and you have conquered the evil one." The implication is that spiritual young men (and women) conquer the devil because of their deep knowledge of Scripture, even as Christ conquered the devil. In contrast, if people are weak in Scripture, they will find themselves more vulnerable to temptation, sin, and the devil.

Paul taught that even the Old Testament narratives were meant to help us battle sin. For example, in 1 Corinthians 10:6-11, Paul said that Israel's grumbling and committing immorality during their wilderness wanderings were included in Scripture "as examples for us, so that we will not crave evil things as they did" (v. 6). Therefore, we should study Scripture to help us conquer sin and temptations from the devil.

People Should Study Scripture to Be Protected from False Teaching

One of the most repeated themes in the New Testament is warnings against false teaching. Christ warned against false teaching (Matt 7:15-20). Most of Paul's letters were written to correct false doctrines that were spreading throughout the church. He also taught that in the last days there would be many demonic teachers and teachings in the church (1 Tim 4:2).

Because of this reality, believers must continually study God's Word to be protected. Paul described immature believers as "children, tossed back and forth by waves and carried about by every wind of teaching by the trickery of people who craftily carry out their deceitful schemes" (Eph 4:14). Just as small children are prone to danger because of lack of wisdom and life experience, so are spiritual children. In order to grow, they must study Scripture. First Peter 2:2 says, "And yearn like newborn infants for pure, spiritual milk, so that by it you may grow up to salvation." By yearning for God's Word (and therefore studying it), believers mature and become less vulnerable to false teaching. In fact, the Berean Christians in Acts 17:11 (NIV) were called "noble" because of their consistent and fervent practice of testing Paul's teaching against Scripture to see if it was true. We must do the same.

People Should Study Scripture to Know and Experience God's Promises

Scripture is full of promises. Some have counted over 3,000 within Scripture. Second Peter 1:3-4 says this about God's promises:

> I can pray this because his divine power has bestowed on us everything necessary for life and godliness through the rich knowledge of the one who called us by his own glory and excellence. Through these things he has bestowed on us his precious and most magnificent promises, so that by means of what was promised you may become partakers of the divine nature, after escaping the worldly corruption that is produced by evil desire.

These promises were given to enable us to participate in the divine nature—which means to make us more like God—and to help us escape the corruption of the world. Some are unconditional, such as God's promise, "I will never leave you and I will never abandon you" (Heb 13:5). However, others are conditional—meaning that we have a role in receiving them.

Here are a few conditional promises to consider. Philippians 4:6-7 says,

> Do not be anxious about anything. Instead, in every situation, through prayer and petition with thanksgiving, tell your requests to God. And the peace of God that surpasses all understanding will guard your hearts and minds in Christ Jesus.

God promises his supernatural peace for those who practice prayer, petition, and thanksgiving in everything they do.

19

When we live out these disciplines, instead of worrying and complaining, God gives us his peace.

First John 1:9 says: "But if we confess our sins, he is faithful and righteous, forgiving us our sins and cleansing us from all unrighteousness." God promises to forgive us when we confess our sins to him; therefore, believers don't have to live in guilt. God is gracious to forgive all our sins when we come to him with repentant hearts.

Proverbs 11:25 says: "whoever refreshes others will be refreshed." Likewise, Christ said, "Blessed are the merciful for they will be shown mercy" (Matt 5:7). This is especially important for those in serving ministries who are prone to burn out and discouragement. This doesn't give them a license to neglect rest and self-care, but it does mean that when they prioritize caring for others, God will care for them.

Scripture is full of God's promises which are meant to change, direct, and comfort us.

People Should Study Scripture to Find Endurance and Encouragement

In Romans 15:4, Paul said, "For everything that was written in former times was written for our instruction, so that through endurance and through encouragement of the scriptures we may have hope." For example, many find great encouragement by reading in the Psalms, how others transparently wrestled with their faith while encountering the trials and worries of life. The Old Testament narratives also often help people endure difficulties, as they consider how others faithfully endured seemingly insurmountable circumstances and how God used those circumstances for good. God used Moses' flight from Egypt as a fugitive and his role as a shepherd in the wilderness for forty years, as preparation for him to lead the Israelite slaves out of slavery in Egypt and shepherd them for forty years in the wilderness. God used the evil Joseph's brothers did against him—selling him into slavery—to create character in Joseph and the circumstances where Joseph would one day rule over Egypt and help many people. We should read Scripture to gain endurance and encouragement to persevere in life's trials.

People Should Study Scripture to Be Empowered by God's Spirit

Consider the following passages: In Ephesians 5:18-20, Paul said:

> And do not get drunk with wine, which is debauchery, but be filled by the Spirit, speaking to one another in psalms, hymns, and spiritual songs, singing and making music in your hearts to the Lord, always giving thanks to God the Father for each other in the name of our Lord Jesus Christ, and submitting to one another out of reverence for Christ.

When Paul commanded believers to be filled with the Spirit, he was challenging them to be continually controlled and empowered by God's Spirit. This is clear from the implied comparison with drunkenness. In the same way wine can control a person, believers should be controlled and empowered by the Spirit. Paul then described the fruits of a Spirit-filled person: a Spirit-filled person worships God by singing psalms, hymns, and spiritual songs. While an unfilled person is consumed with themselves, a filled person is consumed with worshiping God. The filled person is thankful. When unfilled, we are prone to bitterness and grumbling, but when filled, we see God in control of even difficult circumstances, causing us to be thankful. Finally, the filled person submits to others out of reverence to Christ instead of constantly fighting with them and seeking his or her own way. Such

21

submission is accomplished by the power of the Spirit. A Spirit-filled life is a supernatural life.

How then can we be filled with the Spirit—controlled and empowered by him? Consider a parallel passage written by Paul in Colossians 3:16-18,

> Let the word of Christ dwell in you richly, teaching and exhorting one another with all wisdom, singing psalms, hymns, and spiritual songs, all with grace in your hearts to God. And whatever you do in word or deed, do it all in the name of the Lord Jesus, giving thanks to God the Father through him. Wives, submit to your husbands, as is fitting in the Lord.

As believers allow the word of Christ to dwell in them richly, they become teachers, worshipers, Christ-conscious, thankful, and submissive. These characteristics are virtually the same as being filled with the Spirit. This makes perfect sense. Since the Spirit is the author of Scripture, he controls and empowers the person who is filled with God's Word. Unfortunately, many lack power in their Christian life—power to conquer sin, to love others, and to be thankful, regardless of their circumstances—because they are not filled with God's Word and therefore are not filled with God's Spirit.

People Should Study Scripture to Please God and Be Approved by Him

In 2 Timothy 2:15 (NIV), Paul said, "Do your best to present yourself to God as one approved, a worker who does not need to be ashamed and who correctly handles the word of truth." Essentially, Paul said that God approves those who do their best to study and correctly handle God's Word. Therefore, it must be realized that some will ultimately not be approved because of how they neglected and mishandled Scripture.

This is not referring to God rejecting some for salvation, as salvation comes by faith and not by works (Eph 2:8-9). But it certainly refers to being useful to the Lord and rewarded. To some, God will say, "Well done, good and faithful servant!" and reward them (cf. Matt 25:21, 1 Cor 3:14). For others, there will be a loss of reward, based on what they did (or did not do) with God's Word (cf. Matt 5:19, 2 John 1:8, 1 Cor 3:15). We should do our best to study Scripture, rightly apply it, and teach others so we can bring pleasure to God and be approved by him. As Paul said of himself and the apostles, we are all stewards of God's mysteries, who must prove ourselves faithful (1 Cor 4:1-2).

Conclusion

Why do so many Christians struggle with reading and studying Scripture? Maybe, in part, because they have never thought deeply about how great Scripture is and the benefits of studying it, and therefore lack consistent motivation.

1. People Should Study Scripture to Learn About Salvation—How to Have Eternal Life
2. People Should Study Scripture to Grow in Righteousness
3. People Should Study Scripture to Discern God's Direction
4. People Should Study Scripture to Have a Fruitful Life
5. People Should Study Scripture to Conquer Sin and Temptations from the Devil
6. People Should Study Scripture to Be Protected from False Teaching
7. People Should Study Scripture to Know and Experience God's Promises
8. People Should Study Scripture to Find Endurance and Encouragement
9. People Should Study Scripture to Be Empowered by God's Spirit

23

10. People Should Study Scripture to Please God and Be Approved by Him

Reflection

1. In the reading, what reason for studying Scripture stood out most to you and why?
2. Do you struggle with being motivated to study Scripture? If so, why? If not, why not?
3. How have you experienced the benefits of Scripture, including God making you more fruitful, giving you encouragement, endurance, guidance, and the ability to conquer sin?
4. What is your favorite promise in Scripture and why?
5. What are some other, unlisted, benefits of studying Scripture?
6. What other questions or applications do you have from the reading?

Foundations for Understanding Scripture

When constructing a building, builders start by securing a strong foundation. If the foundation is off, the building will have problems and possibly be unsafe. Likewise, when developing a life of studying and understanding Scripture, great attention must be given to the foundation. A faulty foundation will seriously compromise one's study—possibly leading to spiritually injuring oneself and others. Many in the body of Christ have been hurt by a faulty foundation and some have even fallen away from the faith. In this lesson, we will consider six foundations for understanding Scripture.

Foundation 1: We Must Be Born Again to Understand Scripture

The first foundation for understanding the Bible is the necessity of the new nature, which we receive at spiritual birth. Consider what the Bible says about the state of every person before salvation: In 1 Corinthians 2:14, Paul said: "The unbeliever does not receive the things of the Spirit of God, for they are foolishness to him. And he cannot understand them, because they are spiritually discerned." Similarly, in Romans 8:7 (NIV), he said, "The mind governed by the flesh is hostile to God; it does not submit to God's law, nor can it do so."

Paul taught something called human inability. When sin came into the world, it affected people in such a way that, apart from God's grace in salvation, they cannot accept God's Word. Scripture is foolishness to them, and they can't understand it. Apart from saving grace, the world scoffs at a God who created the earth by his Word. They scoff at a God who judged the earth through a world-wide flood. They scoff at God's Son becoming a man, being born of a virgin, dying for the sins of the world, and then being resurrected. Only God's Spirit can give someone grace to accept the things of God. Therefore, people need to be born again to properly interpret Scripture.

How can a person be born again? John said this:

> But to all who have received him—those who believe in his name—he has given the right to become God's children—children not born by human parents or by human desire or a husband's decision, but by God.
> John 1:12-13

When a person receives Christ—believing that Christ died on the cross and rose from the dead for people's sins and commits to following him as Lord and Savior—he or she is spiritually born again. God gives that person the Holy Spirit and a new nature with a desire to study Scripture and a capacity to understand and obey it.

False Teaching

With that said, it should be understood that a lot of false doctrine comes from those within the church who are not truly born again and therefore cannot properly understand Scripture. Consider what Peter said about Paul's scriptural writings:

Bear in mind that our Lord's patience means salvation, just as our dear brother Paul also wrote you with the wisdom that God gave him. He writes the same way in all his letters, speaking in them of these matters. His letters contain some things that are hard to understand, which ignorant and unstable people distort, as they do the other Scriptures, to their own destruction. Therefore, dear friends, since you have been forewarned, be on your guard so that you may not be carried away by the error of the lawless and fall from your secure position.
2 Peter 3:15-17 (NIV)

Peter said that some of Paul's writings were hard to understand and that ignorant and unstable people distorted them, as they did with other Scriptures, to their own destruction. He also said these people were lawless—meaning disobedient to God. In fact, Peter's entire letter is a warning against false teachers. It seems evident that those twisting Scripture "to their own destruction" were not true believers (v. 16).

Christ taught something similar in the Parable of the Weeds and the Wheat (Matt 13:36-43). The parable teaches that in the kingdom there are weeds—false believers—planted by the evil one, and wheat—true believers—planted by God. The apostle John taught something similar when describing the false believers and teachers who left the church of Ephesus. In 1 John 2:19-20, he said:

They went out from us, but they did not really belong to us, because if they had belonged to us, they would have remained with us. But they went out from us to demonstrate that all of them do not belong to us. Nevertheless you have an anointing from the Holy One, and you all know. I have not written to you that you do not know the truth, but that you do know it, and that no lie is of the truth.

John said those who left the church because of accepting heretical doctrine were not saved. He said, "they went out from us, but they did not really belong to us." They were never truly born again. Then John said to the church, "but you have an anointing from the Holy One and you all know" (v. 20). John believed that the true believers in Ephesus were not led astray into heretical teaching because they had an "anointing" from God. This refers to the Holy Spirit. In the Old Testament, the term "anointing" was used for the prophets, priests, and kings who were anointed with oil, conferring upon them the recognition and resources needed for their ministries. When they were anointed, the Spirit came on them to empower them for their work. The work that John referred to is that of interpreting Scripture. True believers have an anointing which teaches them "truth" (v. 20-21) which will keep them from heretical error. Similarly, in John 10, Christ taught that his sheep hear his voice and will not follow the voice of others.

False conversion—not being truly born again—partly explains some of the great heresies infiltrating the church, such as Christ not being God or human, all people will go to heaven, salvation by works, to name a few. Being truly born again is the foundation of understanding Scripture. The person without the Spirit cannot understand or accept the things that come from the Spirit.

This does not mean true Christians will not have different understandings of Scripture, especially on minor doctrines; but in a supernatural way because of their anointing, they will be kept from heretical error which misinterprets the gospel and essential aspects of it.

Have you been born again? Do you have the Holy Spirit's anointing to understand Scripture? With this anointing, one will have a desire to study God's Word and the ability to understand

and obey it (cf. 1 Pet 1:2, Rom 8:7, 1 Cor 2:14-15). This is a proof that one is born again by the Spirit of God, and it is crucial for studying and understanding Scripture.

Foundation 2: We Must Depend on God to Understand Scripture

This corresponds with the first point. In salvation, God enlightens our minds to understand the gospel; however, we must daily learn to live in dependence upon God to continually understand Scripture. In fact, consider what Christ said to the disciples about the Holy Spirit's work in their lives:

> But when he, the Spirit of truth, comes, he will guide you into all truth. For he will not speak on his own authority, but will speak whatever he hears, and will tell you what is to come. He will glorify me, because he will receive from me what is mine and will tell it to you.
> John 16:13-14

The Holy Spirit is the Spirit of truth, and his job is to guide us into truth. In 1 Corinthians 2:12, Paul said: "Now we have not received the spirit of the world, but the Spirit who is from God, so that we may know the things that are freely given to us by God."

Example of the Disciples

We get a good picture of our need to depend on God to correctly study Scripture from the story of Christ talking with his disciples on the road to Emmaus in Luke 24. After Christ's death, the disciples were confused about Jesus. Was he truly God? Why, then, did he die? While they were walking, Christ appeared to them (although they did not recognize him). He began to teach from Scripture, explaining that the messiah had to die and be resurrected. As Christ was teaching, Luke, the narrator, added something special to the story:

> Then he said to them, "These are my words that I spoke to you while I was still with you, that everything written about me in the law of Moses and the prophets and the psalms must be fulfilled." Then he opened their minds so they could understand the scriptures, and said to them, "Thus it stands written that the Christ would suffer and would rise from the dead on the third day
> Luke 24:44-46

Luke said that Christ "opened their minds so they could understand the Scriptures." Though they were saved, Christ still needed to enlighten them so they could understand Scripture. This is just as much a need for us today as it was for Christ's disciples then. How can we depend on God so we can properly interpret Scripture?

1. To depend on God, we must approach Scripture humbly.

James 4:6 says, "God opposes the proud, but he gives grace to the humble." If we approach Scripture confidently because of our educational achievements or spiritual background, we close the door to true understanding. God fights against the proud but gives grace to the humble. A great example of humility is Moses. In Numbers 12:3, it says Moses was the humblest man on the earth; soon after, it says that God spoke to him face to face, unlike with other prophets, to whom God spoke in dreams and visions (v. 6-8). No doubt, Moses' understanding of God's mysteries was connected to his great humility. When we are proud, we depend on ourselves. When we are humble, we depend on God (and others). Therefore, we must confess our pride and confidence and recognize our inability apart from God to understand Scripture.

Are you approaching Scripture humbly or pridefully? Sometimes, the more we learn about God's Word, the more prone we are to pride—hindering our ability to receive. First Corinthians 8:1 says "knowledge puffs up." Therefore, being humble is a discipline we must continually practice by the power of God's Spirit (cf. Gal 5:22-23), especially as we grow in the knowledge of Scripture.

2. We must approach Scripture prayerfully, demonstrating our dependence on God.

Unfortunately, many Christians don't pray when reading Scripture or listening to a sermon, which often robs them of understanding and application. We must ask God to open our minds to his Word and remove any hindrances to understanding and obedience. Consider how David prayed in Psalm 119:

> Open my eyes so I can truly see the marvelous things in your law!
> Psalm 119:18

> Help me to understand what your precepts mean! Then I can meditate on your marvelous teachings.
> Psalm 119:27

> Give me a desire for your rules, rather than for wealth gained unjustly.
> Psalm 119:36

In order to understand Scripture, we must depend totally on God—approaching Scripture humbly and prayerfully. The prideful are blocked from the riches of God's Word—only the humble receive keys to God's rich truths.

Foundation 3: We Must Depend on Mature Believers to Understand Scripture

To understand Scripture deeply, we must not only depend on God but also seek the insight and counsel of mature believers. This is God's ordained method for believers to study and understand Scripture. In Ephesians 4:8, 11-13, Paul said this:

> Therefore it says, "When he ascended on high he captured captives; he gave gifts to men." ... It was he who gave some as apostles, some as prophets, some as evangelists, and some as pastors and teachers, to equip the saints for the work of ministry, that is, to build up the body of Christ, until we all attain to the unity of the faith and of the knowledge of the Son of God—a mature person, attaining to the measure of Christ's full stature.

This passage describes Christ's ascension to heaven and his bestowing gifts upon people. However, it does not itemize a list of gifts. Instead, it lists *gifted people*: apostles, prophets, evangelists, pastors and teachers. By God's providence, these gifted people are God's blessings to his church to help her mature and grow in serving others.

If believers are going to grow in their understanding of God's Word, they must avail themselves of these gifts. They do this by being involved in a good church where the Bible is clearly preached each week, by participating in church small groups where the Bible is discussed, and by reading good Christian books. By doing this, mature believers help other believers better understand God's Word.

Some Christians may say, "We don't need to depend on other believers to understand God's Word because we have the Holy Spirit!" However, the Holy Spirit is the ultimate author of Ephesians 4, which teaches that God's ordained method to train his church is through the teachings of mature believers. The Holy Spirit empowers this process because God has ordained it; therefore, we must take advantage of it, both to learn God's Word and to help others learn as we teach God's Word to others.

Foundation 4: We Must Develop an Obedient Heart to Understand Scripture

In John 7:16-17, Christ said: "...My teaching is not from me, but from the one who sent me. If anyone wants to do God's will, he will know about my teaching, whether it is from God or whether I speak from my own authority."

In this text, the Jews and the Pharisees were testing Jesus. Essentially, they were asking, "Are Jesus' teachings from God or not?" In response, Christ said the only way they could discern if his teachings were authentic was to choose to do God's will. Negatively speaking, if they continued to have a disobedient heart, God would not give them understanding of Christ's teachings.

This principle is true for us as well. Apart from a willingness to obey God's Word, God will not give us understanding. This is especially noteworthy because often we come to Scripture with our own presuppositions and ideas. We are looking to support what we already believe or want to do, which only hinders true understanding. Sometimes, people even approach Scripture like the Pharisees did with Christ—already antagonistic towards what they perceive God is saying through the text. They don't like what Scripture says about this topic or that topic. Sometimes, they even force their presuppositions into the text—making the text say something it doesn't say. An obedient heart is crucial to properly grasp Scripture. Without it, God will not give us understanding.

Disobedience leads to Deception

In fact, a disobedient or antagonistic heart will often lead to deception. In 1 Timothy 4:1-2 (NIV), Paul described the influx of false teachers in the end times and how they originated. He said:

> The Spirit clearly says that in later times some will abandon the faith and follow deceiving spirits and things taught by demons. Such teachings come through hypocritical liars, whose consciences have been seared as with a hot iron.

Paul taught that demons would deceive people who apparently were already living hypocritically, and these same people would espouse demonic lies. Because these people professed Christ but lived in unrepentant sin, their consciences stopped working and they became vulnerable to deception.

The conscience is a natural warning system from God in all people. It is not perfect, as it has been tainted by sin, but it does provide guard rails to our thinking and actions, indicating approval when we do well and disapproval when we do wrong. If we continue to sin, over time the conscience becomes hardened and stops working as it should.

Without the warning system which cautioned that practicing sexual immorality is wrong, lying is wrong, cheating is wrong, abusing people is wrong, these professed believers practiced these sins—making themselves more vulnerable to demonic deceptions. Eventually, they themselves championed and taught various demonic doctrines. A hardened conscience can lead to all types of wrong views and sins.

In the same way that an obedient heart allows the Holy Spirit to bring understanding, a disobedient heart allows demons to bring deception—even leading some to become false prophets and teachers. Satan uses people with twisted consciences to twist God's Word. This is what the Pharisees did—they twisted God's Word to their own benefit and others' demise. Obedience is a critical foundation to knowing God's Word.

What are some applications we can take from our need to have an obedient heart to understand God's Word?

1. We should consider the need for an obedient heart as an encouragement and promise to those who truly want to understand Scripture.

    Christ said, "If anyone wants to do God's will, he will know about my teaching, whether it is from God or whether I speak from my own authority" (John 7:17). There are many difficult doctrines in Scripture and various views about them; however, if we truly want to obey God's will, God promises to give us understanding. We should bring this promise before God as we seek to understand his Word.

2. We should consider the need for an obedient heart as a warning to the disobedient.

    The more we disobey Scripture, the more prone we are to compromise what it says and lead others astray. This should be sobering for every Bible student. Many cult leaders and followers started out in the church and so did many atheists.
    In 1 Timothy 4:16, Paul said, "Be conscientious about how you live and what you teach. Persevere in this, because by doing so you will save both yourself and those who listen to you." Our life and doctrine are inseparable. They affect one another. An ungodly life negatively affects our doctrine, and false doctrine negatively affects our lives. Therefore, we must protect both.

Foundation 5: We Must Develop a Diligent Spirit to Understand Scripture

In 2 Timothy 2:15, Paul said, "Make every effort to present yourself before God as a proven worker who does not need to be ashamed, teaching the message of truth accurately." "Make every effort" can also be translated "be diligent" or "do your best." One of the reasons there is a lot of misinterpretation of Scripture is simply due to laziness. Many come to Scripture apathetically—unwilling to work hard or give their best efforts to understand it—which often results in misinterpretation. This was especially important for Timothy because he was a teacher and his interpretations affected others—both positively and negatively. However, even without being a teacher, our misinterpretations give the devil an open door into our lives and others.

Again, consider the story of the Bereans in Acts 17:11, "Now the Berean Jews were of more noble character than those in Thessalonica, for they received the message with great eagerness and examined the Scriptures every day to see if what Paul said was true." The Bereans are memorialized in Scripture because when taught by Paul, they examined Scripture with "great eagerness" every day to discern what was true. Unfortunately, there are very few noble Christians. Most simply accept what they were taught by parents, friends, pastors, and teachers. Even our best teachers make mistakes and, therefore, must be tested.

It's especially important to be diligent in our study of Scripture because some doctrines are hard to understand (cf. 2 Peter 3:15-16). What is the Trinity? How do we reconcile God's sovereignty and human responsibility? How could Christ be fully God and yet fully human? Though some doctrines are hard to understand, they are still indispensable—bearing blessings for proper interpretation and consequences for misinterpretation. Difficulty in understanding a text or doctrine does not excuse us from diligent pursuit of proper interpretation and application. God even promised special blessings to those who read, heard, and obeyed the words of Revelation, which is probably the most difficult book in the Bible to understand (Rev 1:3).

Working hard to understand Scripture is not only necessary because some teachings are hard to understand, but also because of how pervasive false teaching is in the church. In Matthew 7:13-20, Christ described how hard it was to enter the kingdom of God, and one of the reasons was because there were so many false teachers. There are many on the wide road that leads to destruction instead of the narrow road, in part, because of rampant false teaching. Without working hard to understand God's Word, we are prone to be led astray—even unto damnation.

How can we practice diligence in our study of the Bible, like the Bereans?

1. *To be diligent in our study of Scripture, we must set aside time to study.* It takes time to mine Scripture for its riches. Many can't understand various deep doctrines in Scripture simply because they are not willing to set aside time to do so. What time in your schedule can you dedicate to studying more of God's Word?

2. *To be diligent in our study of Scripture, we must make sacrifices.* Sacrifice implies cost—giving up something we enjoy to prioritize studying God's Word. The cost could be time watching TV, playing video games, time spent on social media, time with friends, or even sleeping. Are you willing to sacrifice to reap the benefits of studying Scripture?

3. *To be diligent in our study of Scripture, we must become zealous.* Zeal is the emotional component of working hard. There is a difference between someone who just shows up to work and someone who shows up and works hard, and part of that difference is zeal. Jeremiah 29:13 (NIV) says, "You will seek me and find me when you seek me with all your heart." If we don't seek God in his Word with all our heart, we will often miss the riches he desires to give us,

in particular, his presence. Are you zealous to understand God's Word? If not, why not?

Foundation 6: We Must Teach Others to Understand Scripture

It has been well-attested that the best way to learn is to teach. We remember 10% of what we hear, 20% of what we read, 70% of what we discuss, and 95% of what we teach. And throughout Scripture, it is clear that God desires every believer to teach in some capacity. In fact, in Hebrews 5:11-12, the author said:

> On this topic we have much to say and it is difficult to explain, since you have become sluggish in hearing. For though you should in fact be teachers by this time, you need someone to teach you the beginning elements of God's utterances. You have gone back to needing milk, not solid food.

The author said that the Jewish Christians should have been teaching others, but they needed to be retaught the basics and couldn't learn deeper theology because of that. That's how many people are in the church today. They have to be continually retaught because they don't retain what they learn.

All believers are called to teach God's Word. Parents should teach their children (Eph 6:4). Older women should teach younger women (Titus 2:3-4). Believers should teach one another in all wisdom (Col 3:16), and they should also teach unbelievers (Matt 28:19-20). If one struggles with identifying whom to teach, he or she should simply find somebody who knows less and teach that person—even if it is a child or an unbeliever. This is the best way to retain what one has learned and learn more.

Conclusion

In this study, we considered six foundations for understanding Scripture. Apart from them, there will be cracks in our foundation which will hinder our ability to understand Scripture, grow in spiritual maturity, and help others. In fact, bad foundations can hurt us and others.

Foundation 1: We Must Be Born Again to Understand Scripture

Foundation 2: We Must Depend on God to Understand Scripture

Foundation 3: We Must Depend on Mature Believers to Understand Scripture

Foundation 4: We Must Develop an Obedient Heart to Understand Scripture

Foundation 5: We Must Develop a Diligent Spirit to Understand Scripture

Foundation 6: We Must Teach Others to Understand Scripture

Reflection

1. In the reading, what foundation stood out most to you and why?
2. Why is being born again so important for properly understanding Scripture?
3. In what ways have you seen or experienced how an obedient heart leads to understanding Scripture and how a disobedient heart hinders understanding and can even lead to deception?

4. Why is it so important to be diligent and work hard in our study of Scripture? How is God calling you to grow in this area?
5. How have you experienced the benefits of teaching others what you learned from the Bible? Who do you feel God is calling you to, specifically, teach in this season?
6. What other questions or applications do you have from the reading?

Hindrances to Studying Scripture

How do we prepare our hearts to study the Bible? One of the ways we do this is by getting rid of every potential hindrance to studying and understanding God's Word. Ezra 7:10 (ESV) says, "For Ezra had set his heart to study the Law of the LORD, and to do it and to teach his statutes and rules in Israel." In the KJV, it is translated that Ezra "prepared his heart."

In Scripture, the heart often refers to the mind, will, and emotions. It is the center of who we are. Proverbs 4:23 says, "Guard your heart with all vigilance, for from it are the sources of life." Our heart affects our jobs, families, friendships, and our relationship with God and his Word. In Matthew 13:1-23, Christ illustrated this in the Parable of the Soils. In it, he described God's Word being sown into the 'soil' of four different hearts—the wayside ground, the rocky ground, the thorny ground, and the good ground. Though each received the Word, only the good ground produced fruit that lasted. Therefore, we also, like farmers, must discern the ground of our heart and prepare it to receive God's Word and produce fruit.

In this lesson, we will consider six hindrances to studying Scripture, which will aid us in preparing the ground of our heart so it can produce maximum fruit.

Hindrance 1: The Unrepentant Heart

James 1:21 says, "So put away all filth and evil excess and humbly welcome the message implanted within you, which is able to save your souls." What's interesting about James' command to get rid of sin is that it implies that God's Word was already in the hearts of the hearers; however, it was ineffective. In order for the Word to change them, they needed to get rid of sin. Sin hinders our ability to truly receive God's Word.

Peter said something similar, "So get rid of all evil and all deceit and hypocrisy and envy and all slander. And yearn like newborn infants for pure, spiritual milk, so that by it you may grow up to salvation" (1 Pet 2:1-2). Since Peter called believers to get rid of sin before commanding them to "yearn" for or "crave" God's Word, the implication is that sin not only stops us from truly receiving God's Word but also from desiring it. Many believers struggle with their appetite for God's Word because they delight in sin and in the world. Likewise, in 1 John 2:15, John said, "Do not love the world or the things in the world. If anyone loves the world, the love of the Father is not in him." There is a principle working in the world system that draws people away from God. It seeks to satisfy people apart from God, and it is utterly antagonistic to him.

Consider this saying: "The Word of God will keep you from sin, or sin will keep you from the Word of God." People's relationship to God's Word is often an indicator of their relationship to sin. A life characterized by not attending church nor participating in a small group (where God's Word is taught), or by not reading God's Word will lead people into sin. When people are living in sin or being drawn to it, they will often stop attending places or doing things where they hear God's Word. Sin is a hindrance to studying God's Word.

Hindrance 2: The Uncommitted Heart

In the Parable of the Soils, Christ said this about the rocky ground:

> The seed sown on rocky ground is the person who hears the word and immediately receives it with joy. But he has

no root in himself and does not endure; when trouble or persecution comes because of the word, immediately he falls away.
Matthew 13:20-21

This type of soil represents people who hear the Word in church, small group, through their personal study, or by some other means, and they accept it joyfully. However, their faithfulness to it lasts only a short time. When trials or persecution come, they quickly fall away. The ground of their heart is shallow, their commitment weak; therefore, they don't continue in obeying God's Word and many ultimately fall away from God.

This is the uncommitted heart. People with an uncommitted heart may look as if they are living a life that honors and prioritizes God. They may study Scripture, attend church, and participate in small groups regularly, but they produce no lasting fruit because of their lack of commitment. They want God and his Word as long as things are good, as long as God is blessing them; but as soon as things go wrong, they fall away from Scripture reading, church attendance, and obedience to God. They may even get angry at God and deny him altogether.

How can we tell if we have an uncommitted heart? Simply by considering how we respond in trials. If we continually get angry at God and run away from him in trials instead of running to him, we have an uncommitted heart, which negatively affects our ability to receive God's Word.

Consider our typical response to one who is uncommitted or untrustworthy: Would we entrust our deepest secrets to someone who is uncommitted or untrustworthy, or give them an important task? No, we wouldn't, because they would probably be unfaithful with it. We can be sure that God doesn't entrust the revelation of his Word to someone who is uncommitted or untrustworthy, either. Psalm 25:14 says, "The LORD's loyal followers receive his guidance, and he reveals his covenantal demands to them." God reveals his Word to his "loyal followers"—not the uncommitted ones. Shallow hearts only get shallow revelation. As they become faithful with little, then God will give them more (cf. Lk 16:10). When they are unfaithful with little, God takes away even what they have (cf. Matt 13:12). The uncommitted heart is a hindrance to studying God's Word.

Hindrance 3: The Worrying Heart

In Matthew 13:22 (NIV), Christ described the thorny ground and how worry kept this type of heart from fruitfulness. In explaining it, Christ said, "The seed falling among the thorns refers to someone who hears the word, but the worries of this life ... choke the word, making it unfruitful."

Some of the most frequent commands in Scripture are, "Don't be afraid," "Do not worry," or "Be anxious for nothing." What is wrong with worrying? Worry essentially says to God either "I don't trust you!" or "You are not in control!" However, Scripture tells us that God works all things according to the counsel of his will (Eph 1:11) and that he specifically works all things for the good of those who love him (Rom 8:28). Though hard things happen in our lives, God is always in control and using them for our good; therefore, we must trust him.

Consider this from a human relationship standpoint: if we don't trust somebody, then that distrust will affect what we give them or accept from them. Similarly, how can we expect God to teach us his Word if we don't trust him? One of the prominent themes of Scripture is our need for faith—for us to trust God. We need to put our faith in God for salvation (Eph 2:8-9), but we also need to put our trust in him to receive many of his promises. In Mark 9:23, Christ said to a father seeking healing for his child, "All things are possible for the one who believes." Since fear is basically a lack of faith, it prohibits our ability to receive God's promises and his Word.

45

In reality, many people faithfully spend time in God's Word, yet God's Word is ineffective in their lives because of their propensity to worry. They constantly worry about their future, their past, their relationships, and everything else. Consequently, their worry chokes God's Word and makes it unfruitful (Matt 13:22). Therefore, if we are going to prepare our hearts to study God's Word, we must resolve not to worry but instead to pray, give God thanks, and trust him. Philippians 4:6-7 says,

> Do not be anxious about anything. Instead, in every situation, through prayer and petition with thanksgiving, tell your requests to God. And the peace of God that surpasses all understanding will guard your hearts and minds in Christ Jesus.

And 1 Thessalonians 5:16-18 says, "Always rejoice, constantly pray, in everything give thanks. For this is God's will for you in Christ Jesus."

Hindrance 4: The Materialistic Heart

When describing the thorny ground which didn't produce fruit from God's Word, Christ not only mentioned worry, but also the deceitfulness of wealth as a hindrance. Again, Matthew 13:22 (NIV) says, "The seed falling among the thorns refers to someone who hears the word, but … the deceitfulness of wealth choke the word, making it unfruitful."

This seems to be one of the temptations that kept Eve from obeying God's Word. Though Eve had everything in the world, Satan focused her attention on the one thing that she didn't have—the fruit of the forbidden tree. She looked at the fruit, lusted for it, and ate it—disobeying God's Word.

Since then, "the deceitfulness of wealth" (or materialism) has been a major hindrance to studying and obeying God's Word.

Christ declared that a person can only have one master, God or Money; otherwise, the person will hate one and love the other (Matt 6:24). Christ also emphasized how hard it was for a rich man to get into heaven (Matt 19:23). We are often deceived by wealth. We are tempted to think that it will ultimately satisfy us, so we pursue it more than God. Paul taught Timothy that many had pierced themselves with many sorrows because of the love of wealth and some had even fallen away from the faith (1 Tim 6:9-11).

For this reason, if we are going to prepare our hearts to study God's Word, we must guard against materialism—loving things more than God and others. It's very easy for money, clothes, cars, and electronics to become our idols—hindering our love for God's Word, our ability to understand it, and our desire to obey it.

How can we protect our hearts from materialism? By being obedient to God in these ways: (1) Christ taught that we should not store up treasures on earth, because they are temporary and tend to consume our hearts, but to instead store up treasures in heaven, which are eternal (Matt 6:19-21). Likewise, Paul taught that we should guard our hearts from being "engrossed" with the things of this world (1 Cor 7:31 NIV). To live in the world, we must use things (cars, phones, laptops, Internet, money), but we must guard against being engrossed in them. Sometimes that means not acquiring them, giving them away, or simply being disciplined with them. (2) We are to practice contentment. In 1 Timothy 6:6-8, Paul said if we have food and covering, we should be "content." Contentment is a spiritual discipline we must learn and practice. It often starts with simply giving God thanks for what we have and choosing to not pursue more than what we have. Unfortunately, since our hearts are so deceitful, many are unaware of how consumed their hearts are with material things and how that idolatry has hindered their ability to desire, study, and obey God's Word.

Do you have a materialistic heart? Christ said we can only have one master—God or money. We will love one and hate the other. In order to study God's Word, we must love God and be careful of materialism, which can choke God's Word and render it ineffective.

Hindrance 5: The Busy Heart

Another common hindrance that keeps many from knowing and receiving God's Word is simply busyness. We get a good picture of this in the Mary and Martha story in Luke 10. In the story, Jesus visited Mary and Martha's home. While there, Jesus was teaching and sharing God's Word with the disciples. Mary sat with them and listened while Martha was the 'good' hostess—working feverishly to serve everybody. Eventually, Martha complained to Jesus and asked him to tell Mary to help with serving. Jesus replied: "Martha, Martha, you are worried and troubled about many things, but one thing is needed. Mary has chosen the best part; it will not be taken away from her" (Lk 10:41-42).

Likewise, many people won't study Scripture simply because they are too busy. Often what keeps them away from studying God's Word are not bad things; they can be very good things like school, work, family, or hobbies. However, often the enemy of the best thing is not the evil but the good. No doubt, this is why Paul prayed this for the Philippians:

> And I pray this, that your love may abound even more and more in knowledge and every kind of insight so that you can decide what is best, and thus be sincere and blameless for the day of Christ, filled with the fruit of righteousness that comes through Jesus Christ to the glory and praise of God.
> Philippians 1:9-11

48

As people made in the image of God, we have a tremendous capacity to love; however, our love must be wise. We must be able to discern what is best so we can be holy, fruitful, and bring maximum glory to God.

Is busyness keeping you from studying God's Word and receiving all the benefits which come from it, including fruitfulness? Be careful of the hindrance of the busy heart.

Hindrance 6: The Sectarian (or Denominational) Heart

The sectarian or denominational heart is the believers' tendency to exalt a leader, church, or denomination to the point that it hinders their ability to rightly interpret and obey Scripture. This tendency has plagued the church since its inception and even before the church was formed. In 1 Corinthians 3:1-5, Paul rebuked the Corinthians for unduly exalting their teachers:

> So, brothers and sisters, I could not speak to you as spiritual people, but instead as people of the flesh, as infants in Christ. I fed you milk, not solid food, for you were not yet ready. In fact, you are still not ready, for you are still influenced by the flesh. For since there is still jealousy and dissension among you, are you not influenced by the flesh and behaving like unregenerate people? For whenever someone says, "I am with Paul," or "I am with Apollos," are you not merely human? What is Apollos, really? Or what is Paul? Servants through whom you came to believe, and each of us in the ministry the Lord gave us.

This same heart tendency is demonstrated by Joshua in his reverence for Moses. In Numbers 11:28-29, two men were prophesying in the Israelite camp and Joshua responded: "'My lord Moses, stop them!' Moses said to him, 'Are you jealous for me? I

49

wish that all the LORD's people were prophets, that the LORD would put his Spirit on them!'"

Similarly, we have a propensity to divide into factions around great leaders, churches, and denominations and to become jealous to protect them, even when they are potentially in error. When we overly-reverence them, we risk becoming blind to their flaws. Our idolization hinders our ability to rightly understand and apply God's Word. Robert West in his book, *How to Study the Bible*, gives a challenging warning against overly exalting our teachers, which can also be applied to our churches and denominations:

> Christians must also beware of becoming -ites. These are believers who automatically accept everything that a certain Christian author says or writes. Using the names of popular contemporary Christian authors, these people could be known as Swindollites, Lucadoites, or LaHayeites.[i]

Though God uses great teachers and leaders to help us grow, we must remember they still have clay feet—they stumble and make mistakes, including misinterpreting Scripture. Certainly, this is also true with churches and denominations. None of them have a patent on the truth. With that said, we should allow God to use our teachers, churches, and denominations to help us learn truth. However, we must, like the Bereans, test everything taught (and practiced) by comparing it to God's Word (Acts 17:11), holding fast to the good and discarding the bad.

As an application, we must continually come before Scripture with an open heart and mind—trying to honestly discern what Scripture says, even if it differs from what we've previously learned or accepted. We must recognize that only God's Word is infallible—not ourselves, our culture, great leaders, churches, or denominations.

Conclusion

Even as Ezra prepared his heart to study Scripture, we must do the same. We must get rid of every potential hindrance to studying and obeying Scripture. As Proverbs 4:23 says, we must guard our hearts, for out of them flow the issues of life. We must be especially careful of hindrances like:

1. The Unrepentant Heart
2. The Uncommitted Heart
3. The Worrying Heart
4. The Materialistic Heart
5. The Busy Heart
6. The Sectarian (or Denominational) Heart

Reflection

1. In the reading, what hindrance stood out most to you and why?
2. How have you seen or experienced this saying, "The Bible will either keep you from sin, or sin will keep you from the Bible"?
3. Why is worry such a hindrance to understanding and obeying God's Word? In what ways do you struggle with worry? How can we protect ourselves from this hindrance?
4. Why is busyness such a hindrance to understanding and obeying God's Word? How can we protect ourselves from this hindrance?
5. How have you seen or experienced the sectarian heart? What is the remedy for this negative tendency?
6. What other questions or applications do you have from the reading?

Bible Study Tools

When you come, bring with you the cloak I left in Troas
with Carpas and the scrolls, especially the parchments.
2 Timothy 4:13

What types of resources does one need to study the Bible?

If you visited the home of someone who is great at
something, typically you would find that he or she would have
collected many tools and resources related to their hobby or craft.
Great fishermen will have an assortment of fishing rods, types of
lures, the appropriate clothes, and possibly even a boat. Great
musicians will have a collection of instruments, sheet music,
perhaps electronic equipment, and the like. Great businessmen will
have books on leadership, marketing, and maybe even statistics.
Similarly, people who are going to go deep in their study and
understanding of the Bible will also need a collection of helpful
resources.

In fact, many believe that 2 Timothy 4:13 mentions the
tools of the greatest apostle. When Paul asked for "parchments,"
he was probably asking for the Hebrew Scriptures, which were
often written on bark or animal skins. The "scrolls" were very likely
parts of the New Testament and other resources used to study
Scripture. There were many Jewish writings on the Old Testament
which Paul, as a Pharisee, would have had at his disposal.
Presumably, these were the resources that he was requesting.
Charles Spurgeon used this passage to rebuke pastors who
preached but neglected study. He said this of Paul:

He is inspired, and yet he wants books! He has been preaching at least for thirty years, and yet he wants books! He had seen the Lord, and yet he wants books! He had had a wider experience than most men, and yet he wants books! He had written the major part of the New Testament, and yet he wants books![ii]

To study God's Word deeply, Christians should seriously consider developing their libraries.

Needing Resources Outside of the Bible

Now some would automatically reject this and say, "All we need is our Bibles for study!" However, for at least two reasons, outside resources are needed for deeper study: (1) The first reason is that the Bible is an ancient manuscript. We need to know the historical background and culture, which is often different from ours, to properly understand the text. Resources outside the Bible will help with that. (2) And secondly, God has chosen to mature his church through gifted people teaching the Word. In Ephesians 4:11-12, Paul said this:

It was he who gave some as apostles, some as prophets, some as evangelists, and some as pastors and teachers, to equip the saints for the work of ministry, that is, to build up the body of Christ,

Often people rely on God to equip the church only through the oral instruction given by teachers in Sunday service or Bible study. This is certainly part of God's plan to edify and instruct his people; however, God also builds the church through the writings of gifted teachers. In fact, God chose to build up the church not only through the oral teachings of the apostles but specifically through their writings—many of which are now known as Scripture.

God, by his grace, has equipped many great teachers to write about Scripture to aid the church in understanding his Word. Unlike the Bible, these resources are not inspired, and as such, should never replace Scripture. But, properly used, they can greatly supplement our studies and help us understand the Bible better.

Like Paul, we must use our "scrolls" to help us understand the Bible—the historical background, the ancient culture, the nuances of the original languages, how a specific text corresponds with the rest of Scripture, etc.

Types of Tools

What types of tools should Christians use to help them understand Scripture better? It should be noted that many of these resources can be found on the Internet for free. However, one will have to spend some money to adequately expand their library.

1. Multiple Bible Translations

As mentioned, when Paul asked for the parchments, he was probably referring to the Old Testament, of which there were multiple versions. Often when Paul or other NT writers quoted the Old Testament, they quoted the Septuagint—the OT Greek translation. Other times, they used the Hebrew translation. Similarly, reading and referencing multiple translations will aid our understanding of Scripture, as well.

Multiple translations are helpful because one translation alone cannot fully capture the meaning of a word in the original Hebrew or Greek. For instance, in English there is one word for 'love," but in Greek, there are at least four, each depicting distinct types and characteristics of love. Sometimes by using different translations and comparing them, it helps us have a fuller understanding of a given word or verse.

It has often been asked, "What is the best Bible translation?" The simple answer is, "Whatever one you will read!" There are many versions: The English Standard Version, the New American Standard, the New King James, the NIV, the NET, among others, are all rich translations, which benefit readers in some way or another.

The below online resources provide multiple Bible translations for study:

- http://biblehub.com/
- http://www.biblegateway.com/
- http://www.e-sword.net/ (on E-sword you will have to download various versions)

2. A Study Bible

Why is a study Bible so important? A study Bible minimizes one's need for multiple resources. The first few pages of each book in a study Bible includes introductory material: author, original audience, historical background, the purpose of the book, etc. Surveying the introductory material of a Bible book before reading the book is like surveying the forest before looking at each tree—it will often enrich one's Bible reading.

In the center of each study Bible page, there are Scripture cross-references for each verse. When you read a verse on divorce (cf. Matt 5:31-32), several similar verses are provided (cf. Matt 18: 3-9, 1 Cor 7:10-14), which will enhance one's understanding of the particular passage or the topic within the passage you are reading. A study Bible also has small commentary for many of the verses in a chapter. Do you ever look at a verse and say, "What does that mean?" The commentary will often provide both insight and application. Also, a study Bible will have a small concordance where one can look up verses by simply remembering key words in the passage. Here are four recommended study Bibles:

- The ESV Study Bible
- John MacArthur's Study Bible
- The Life Application Study Bible
- The NIV Study Bible

3. Commentaries

Comments in a study Bible will be concise; however, commentary volumes will give a more thorough explanation of each verse. These are especially helpful for not only comprehending verses but for preparation to teach them. Often commentaries lead the reader from asking the question "What does this mean?" to "What do we *do* about it?" This is especially true of commentaries made for personal devotions and for helping pastors prepare to teach. Purchasing one or more commentaries for each Bible book is costly; however, there are free high-quality commentaries online, as well as good single volume commentaries for purchase. Some examples of both are below:

- Matthew Henry's Complete Commentary (free online)
- Enduring Word Commentary by David Guzik (free online)
- The Free Bible Commentary by Bob Utley (free online)
- Believers Bible Commentary by William MacDonald
- The MacArthur Bible Commentary
- The Warren Wiersbe OT Commentary and NT Commentary

Likewise, there are many good commentary series with single volumes of various Bible books. For example, *The Preaching the Word* series, *The Tyndale Commentaries*, *The MacArthur New*

Testament series, and *The Bible Teacher's Guide* series. With that said, it should be noted that not all commentaries are created equal. Some are written by liberal scholars with a naturalistic bend—meaning that they don't believe in miracles, such as the resurrection. Some are academic—focusing on the original languages, which might be hard to understand without language training. Each commentary will reflect the theological persuasion of the author (Reformed, Arminian, Dispensational, Lutheran, etc.). Nonetheless, God has especially gifted commentators from various theological persuasions to write certain books or a series of books. To discern the best commentaries, it is wise to consider reviews, get counsel, and if possible, read portions of the commentary before purchasing.

4. Systematic Theologies

Unlike commentaries, which focus on a single Bible book and verses within it, systematic theologies teach what the whole Bible says about major topics like God the Father, the Holy Spirit, Jesus, salvation, angels, and eschatology (end times). Within those major topics, they cover sub-topics, including the Trinity, God's sovereignty, election, the security of a believer, and demons. There are many fine systematic theologies available: Wayne Grudem's *Systematic Theology* (and the smaller version, *Bible Doctrine*), Millard Erickson's *Christian Theology* (and the smaller version, *Introducing Christian Doctrine*), and Charles Ryrie's *Basic Theology*, among others.

5. A Bible Concordance and Dictionary

A concordance is helpful for locating passages in the Bible. It indexes Bible words in alphabetical order—allowing people to find verses they are looking for by only remembering a key word in a certain passage. Concordances are based on specific Bible translations; therefore, looking up words from the KJV in a NIV concordance might not be very helpful. The indexed words in a concordance are also often connected to the original language equivalent—allowing a person to look up the exact meaning in Hebrew, Greek, or Aramaic. A popular concordance based on the KJV is _Strong's Exhaustive Concordance_. Additionally, if a significant portion of a passage is entered online, search engines like Google and Yahoo can function like concordances, when those phrases are searched.

6. Other Tools

There are many other great Bible tools including biblical encyclopedias, which have hundreds of articles about topics in Scripture, Bible atlases, which help with understanding the geography in Bible times, and Bible surveys, which provide an overview of every book in the Bible. If we are going to thoroughly study Scripture, like Paul, we need our "scrolls" and "parchments" (2 Tim 4:13). Do you have yours?

Reflection

1. In the reading, what stood out most to you and why?
2. Are tools outside the Bible necessary to study the Bible? Why or why not?
3. Which Bible tools are you most familiar with and how have you found them helpful?
4. Is there a specific tool you are most interested in trying?
5. What other questions or applications do you have from the reading?

Bible Study Skills: OIL

When studying the Bible, an important acronym to remember is OIL: Observation, Interpretation, Life application. Observation asks this question about a passage, "What does it say?" Interpretation asks, "What does it mean?" Life Application asks, "What should we do about it?" Only after diligently analyzing a passage can one truly find its meaning, and only after understanding the meaning of a passage can one properly apply it. Observing, interpreting, and applying are skills which the Bible student must develop to become competent at studying Scripture. We will look at each skill separately.

Observation

A popular genre of film and books is criminal scene investigation (CSI). CSI stories follow a regimented procedure: after a crime is committed and discovered, the police isolate the crime scene to make sure no one tampers with evidence. Then, investigators screen the area for items such as blood, hair, broken glass, bubble gum, and receipts. They do this because they realize that any detail, even a tiny detail that seems insignificant, might lead to solving the crime. Like an investigator meticulously studying a crime scene for clues, Bible students must learn to develop a similar procedure when studying Scripture. Several components are necessary for a Bible student to do this:

Believe That All Scripture Matters

First, Bible students must believe that all Scripture matters—even seemingly insignificant details. Consider the following verses:

Every scripture is inspired by God and useful for teaching, for reproof, for correction, and for training in righteousness, that the person dedicated to God may be capable and equipped for every good work.
2 Timothy 3:16-17

But he answered, "It is written, 'Man does not live by bread alone, but by every word that comes from the mouth of God.
Matthew 4:4

Second Timothy 3:16 tells us that "every" or "all" Scripture is inspired, not "some." Jesus stated that we live by "every" word that comes from the mouth of God. In fact, in Matthew 5:18, Christ said this: "I tell you the truth, until heaven and earth pass away not the smallest letter or stroke of a letter will pass from the law until everything takes place." These verses emphasize that every portion of Scripture is important—even the smallest letter and stroke of a letter. This realization is vital to developing the skill of observation. God chose the specific words, including tenses, in a passage for a purpose. Therefore, we must develop keen vision to notice details and seek to understand what the Holy Spirit, through human authors, was trying to say to the original audience and now to the contemporary audience.

We can discern the importance of every word and how it can lead to both meaning and application by observing how Christ confronted the Sadducees' lack of belief in the resurrection in Matthew 22:30-32. He said:

For in the resurrection they neither marry nor are given in marriage, but are like angels in heaven. Now as for the resurrection of the dead, have you not read what was spoken to you by God, 'I am the God of Abraham, the God of Isaac, and the God of Jacob'? He is not the God of the dead but of the living!" When the crowds heard this, they were amazed at his teaching.

Christ asked, "have you not read what was spoken to you by God, 'I am the God of Abraham, the God of Isaac, and the God of Jacob'?" Surely the Pharisees had read it before, just as most

Christians have, but what made Christ's reading of this OT text so different was his keen observation of it. Christ pointed out that though Abraham, Isaac, and Jacob were dead, the original writer wrote about them in the present tense, which meant they were still alive and therefore would be resurrected.

Believing in the importance of every aspect of Scripture is indispensable. If we don't believe that all of Scripture is important, we might skip certain parts (like genealogies or historical details) or not read God's Word at all. If we're going to develop observation skills, we must believe that "all Scripture is God-breathed," that we are called to live by "every word" of God, and that even the smallest letter and least stroke of the pen will never pass away. Just as Christ asked the Sadducees, we must ask ourselves, "Have we truly been reading?"

What else is needed to properly observe Scripture?

Become Spiritually Inquisitive

To properly observe Scripture, we must become spiritually inquisitive. We must ask questions about the Bible and its passages. Many can't understand Scripture deeply merely because they're not interested in knowing the meaning and application of Scripture. They're simply content to read it, if that. This is part of the reason why, in 1 Peter 2:2, Peter commanded believers to "yearn" for "spiritual milk" like an infant. People won't need to be told to read the Bible, memorize it, and study it, if they actually "yearn" for it. Yearning will motivate us to do all those things. Therefore, God commands us to have a hungry disposition, as we will need it to understand Scripture and grow from it.

Certainly, we see this inquisitive, hungry disposition in the disciples, who often asked Christ questions about his teachings. For example, consider the disciples' interaction with Christ after he taught the Parable of the Sowers in Luke 8:8-9:

But other seed fell on good soil and grew, and it produced a hundred times as much grain." As he said this, he called out, "The one who has ears to hear had better listen!" Then his disciples asked him what this parable meant.

After presenting the parable, Jesus added, "The one who has ears to hear had better listen!" This meant that not everybody was capable of understanding the parable—including his own disciples! However, their desire to understand it and their request for Christ to explain it was proof that they had ears to hear. Sadly, most people read passages in the Bible without any understanding and simply move on to the next verse. They don't ask questions of the text, pray about it, or research it further. Having "ears to hear" doesn't just mean we understand Scripture when we read it; it means we desire understanding and are willing to pursue it. This separated the disciples from the rest of the hearers in Luke 8:8-9, who didn't understand the parable either but failed to pursue further explanation.

As we read the Gospels, the inquisitive nature of the apostles continues to be displayed. After Christ taught the need to pursue reconciliation with those who sinned against us, Peter asked, "Lord, how many times must I forgive my brother who sins against me? As many as seven times?" (Matt 18:21). Similarly, after Christ taught the disciples about the destruction of the temple in Matthew 24:3, they asked him privately, "Tell us, when will these things happen? And what will be the sign of your coming and of the end of the age?"

One might say, "We don't have Christ here to ask questions of the Bible. How do we get further understanding of his words, and the Bible's teachings in general, like the disciples did?" In John 14:16-17, Christ said this to the disciples, after telling them that he would be leaving them: "Then I will ask the Father, and he will give you another Advocate [or Counselor] to be with you forever—the Spirit of truth." Christ used an interesting word to refer to the Holy Spirit. Two Greek words are typically used for "another." One means "another of a different kind," and the other is "another of the same kind." Christ used the latter. Essentially, Christ said to his disciples, "I will send you someone just like me. I will not leave you as orphans. I will send the Holy Spirit to you. He will teach you the truth and explain things to you. He will be your counselor. In the same way, you asked me questions, ask him questions." Christ has given us this Counselor as well—the Spirit of truth. He will lead us into all truth, as we depend on him.

Therefore, it must be understood that those who don't prayerfully ask questions of the Bible—trying to understand its meaning and applications—will not grow in understanding it. Like the multitudes who listened to Christ while never understanding his words, so is the person who reads Scripture and listens to sermons, yet never asks questions or pursues answers. Again, Christ said, "The one who has ears to hear had better listen!" The person who has ears is the one with an inquisitive nature—who genuinely wants to understand and obey God's Word.

What should we do if we don't desire to read and understand God's Word?

1. Repent of not desiring to know God. Repent of not desiring to understand his Word. Repent of desiring and prioritizing so many other things above God and his Word.

2. Pray for God to give you a hunger to read and understand God's Word. In Psalm 119:36, David prayed, "Give me a desire for your rules, rather than for wealth gained unjustly." He prayed for his desire and so must we.

3. Begin to read Scripture, ask questions of the text, and pursue those answers.

Ask Questions of Scripture

As we become spiritually inquisitive, we must ask questions of Scripture as we study it, such as:

- ✓ Who
- ✓ What
- ✓ Why
- ✓ When
- ✓ Where
- ✓ How

These questions are fundamental to reading in general; however, it is helpful to write the questions down and routinely ask them while reading the Bible, until this becomes a natural habit. For example:

> *Who:* Who is the author of the text? Who was this text originally written to?

> *What:* What exactly is being said? What does the writing mean? What is the theme or purpose of the writing? What is the historical background? What type of writing is this—narrative, prophecy, letter, sermon, song, prayer, quotation, etc.? What is the immediate context of the passage?

> *Why:* Why was this written? Are there any purpose clauses (these typically begin with *so, because, to, for, so that*, etc., which help discern the author's purpose in writing a specific text)?

When: When was this written or when will this promise be fulfilled? Are there any time references in the text such as before, after, until, then, etc.?

Where: Where was this text written? Where is the narrative taking place?

How: How does this passage connect with other teachings in Scripture? How should this passage be applied? How should I pray from this passage?

Develop an Eye for Details

While reading the text and asking questions, take note of details which may provide answers to the questions or prompt further questions. Specifically, focus on details such as:

- literary genre (narrative, poetry, prophecy, epistle, etc.)
- grammatical structure of a sentence or paragraph
- key words
- things emphasized by repetition, amount of space given to it, or the order (sometimes order shows priority)
- comparisons
- contrasts
- cause and effect
- explanations
- commands
- exaggerations
- foreshadowing
- promises
- applications
- doctrine
- going from specific to general (or vice versa)

- the end of a scene
- the plot
- the climax

As one practices searching passages for details, his or her eyes will begin to readily pick up noteworthy aspects that lead to interpretation and application. Secondary tools (like commentaries and systematic theologies) will help with training one's eyes to do this, continually pointing the person back to specific aspects of the text and their meaning/application.

Find the Answers by Research

As these questions are asked and details are noticed, they will often inspire the Bible student to further research. This research might lead to reading the text over and over again, reading the surrounding text to establish context, consulting a study Bible or commentary, or directing questions to a more knowledgeable believer. Eventually, if not immediately, these practices will reveal the meaning of the text (interpretation) and how to apply it (life application).

Observation Tips

What are some tips to help with observation?

1. *Saturate the study of Scripture with prayer.* In Psalm 119:18, David said, "Open my eyes so I can truly see the marvelous things in your law!" Like David, we should ask God to open our eyes before studying his Word and while studying it. We should also pray for grace to live out the truths learned from Scripture.

2. *Read the text over and over again (including the surrounding context).* Psalm 1:1-2 (NIV) describes how God blesses the person who delights in and meditates on God's Word. The Hebrew word for "meditate" was used of a cow chewing her cud. A cow has a four-chambered stomach, and because of that, she chews, swallows, and regurgitates over and over again as the food works its way through each chamber. Cows do this in order to maximize extraction of nutrients. Similarly, we'll find as we prayerfully re-read Scripture over and over again that God blesses such study. The Holy Spirit will extract maximum nutrients from the text to edify us. In referring back to the crime scene investigator illustration, often the investigator realizes that he's missing something and, therefore, revisits the crime scene to look for further clues. We must also do that as we study God's Word. And since Scripture is living and active (Heb 4:12), we will find that God continually meets us in the text, no matter how many times we've read it before.

3. *Allow secondary materials to be secondary.* The Bible is the primary source and the Holy Spirit is the guide. Consider commentaries, systematic theologies, Bible dictionaries, and any other secondary material, only after prayerfully meditating on the text. Allow the Bible tools to refocus one's eyes on the text in a fresh way, in order to aid in finding meaning and application.

Conclusion

Are you prayerfully observing God's Word—meditating on it to extract all the nutrients for your spiritual health? Or, are you simply reading Scripture, quickly skimming it, or neglecting it all together? If we are going to understand God's Word, we must believe that all Scripture matters, develop a spiritually inquisitive nature, prayerfully ask questions of the text, begin to notice details, and research for answers. These are critical steps in discerning meaning and then applying it.

Reflection

1. In the reading, what aspect about observing Scripture stood out most to you and why?
2. How can we develop an inquisitive nature—one that seeks to understand and obey Scripture?
3. What types of questions should we ask when studying Scripture?
4. What types of details should we look for when studying the text?
5. What other questions or applications do you have from the reading?

Interpretation

After observing Scripture—considering what it says—one must interpret what it means. The science of Bible interpretation is called biblical hermeneutics. People may think that understanding the Bible is something mystical, but it is not. Hermeneutics is something we do every time we read a newspaper, article, or letter. We are simply using interpretation principles to discern what the author meant when writing to a specific audience. A text generally has one meaning (interpretation), though it may have many applications. The primary difference when interpreting Scripture as compared to secular writings, is the fact that the Bible is God's Word and therefore is without error. Consequently, when confronting seemingly conflicting texts or ideas in the Bible, the interpreter must find out how the texts or truths work together or harmonize without contradicting one another.

Below are hermeneutical principles which will help us understand the meanings of biblical texts:

1. The Literal Principle (or KISS)

Possibly, the most important hermeneutic principle is to read Scripture "literally"—according to the plain or normal sense. It's been said that "if the plain sense makes good sense, seek no other sense, lest one make nonsense." Or, a humorous way to memorize this principle is with the acronym KISS—Keep It Simple Stupid! When the text is symbolic or meant to be a figure of speech, it is clear by the context. For example, poetry (like the Psalms) commonly employs symbols and figures of speech. Apocalyptic literature (prophetic literature about the end of the world) like Revelation, Ezekiel, or Daniel also uses symbols. However, historical literature and epistles do not. In general, stick to the plain sense unless the context demands otherwise.

Here are a few ways to identify symbols. (1) Often the writers of Scripture will introduce a symbol and then provide the literal meaning of it. For example, Revelation 1:16 says, "He held seven stars in his right hand, and a sharp double-edged sword extended out of his mouth…" Revelation 1:20 tells us that the stars refer to churches. (2) Sometimes, the context necessitates a symbolic or metaphoric interpretation by contradicting other Scriptural truths. For example, Psalm 91:4 says this about God, "He will shelter you with his wings; you will find safety under his wings. His faithfulness is like a shield or a protective wall." God having wings is clearly a metaphor because Scripture tells us that God is spirit and, therefore, has no physical body (John 4:24, cf. Lk 24:39). (3) Other times the symbolism is clear because of the impossibility of a literal reading. For example, Psalm 98:8 says, "Let the rivers clap their hands! Let the mountains sing in unison." The author is obviously using symbols of fantastic joy over God and his works (cf. Ps 98:1)!

At times throughout history, interpreters carefully sought hidden, spiritual meanings behind every text—rendering the Bible almost impossible to understand. For example, a tree represented obedience, a river represented the Holy Spirit, and fruit represented evil. Be wary of these types of interpretations, which are not clearly supported in the immediate context. Hermeneutics protects against these types of readings, just as it does with all literature. Again, when interpreting Scripture, keep it simple by using the literal principle, unless the context necessitates otherwise.

2. The Historical Principle

Each portion of Scripture must be understood in its original historical setting, including the author, audience, cultural background, place, and the situation that prompted the writing of the text. Many errors in interpretation occur simply because the reader interpreted according to his or her own experiences and cultural understanding. However, proper Bible interpretation seeks to understand Scripture in the way the original audience would have understood it. Consequently, interpretations that the original audience would not have concluded are likely incorrect. At times, the Holy Spirit, through a different author, reveals to us that a historical person, event, or object was a type of Christ or had some deeper meaning which the original audience wouldn't have discerned. Generally speaking, the historical and cultural setting is key to proper interpretation.

For example, in Matthew 5:29-30, Christ said this about defeating lust:

> If your right eye causes you to sin, tear it out and throw it away! It is better to lose one of your members than to have your whole body thrown into hell. If your right hand causes you to sin, cut it off and throw it away! It is better to lose one of your members than to have your whole body go into hell.

How would the disciples have understood Christ's words about tearing out one's eye and cutting off one's hand? Are there historical equivalents that might help with interpretation? In that historical setting, Christ's words were war terminology. For victors, it was common practice to take prisoners of war. Typically, the prisoners would be maimed or blinded so they could never attack the victors again. That is why the Philistines blinded Samson after defeating him. By blinding him, they aimed to guarantee that Samson would never be able to attack them again. The Babylonians also did this with the Jewish king, Zedekiah; they blinded him and kept him imprisoned until his death (Jer 52:11). However, since tearing out one's eye and cutting off one's hand would not keep a person from lusting (what about the other eye and hand?), it is clear that Christ's words were metaphoric. Christ taught that believers should get rid of anything they were looking at (symbolized by eyes) and anything they were doing (symbolized by hands) which provoked them to lust. Understanding the historical/cultural context helps with interpreting Christ's words.

Another example of the importance of the historical principle is seen in the story of Jonah. God told Jonah to go to Nineveh and call the Assyrians to repent. However, Jonah rebelled against God's Word and fled in the opposite direction. To better understand the narrative, knowing the history between Israel and Assyria is crucial. These nations were bitter enemies. In fact, Assyria would some decades later conquer the Israelites and force them into exile. The nations' histories show us why Jonah despised the Assyrians so much and longed for their destruction. Additionally, understanding their histories also makes Assyria's repentance at Jonah's preaching even more miraculous.

A good Bible student by necessity must be a good historian. Commentaries and other tools will help with this, but the more one is familiar with the whole counsel of Scripture (from Genesis to Revelation), the more the ancient culture becomes familiar, leading to more accurate interpretations.

3. The Contextual Principle

The contextual principle means we must interpret Scripture in its literary context. This is extremely important because without considering the literary context of a verse, one could interpret it to mean essentially anything. For example, Philippians 4:13 says, "I am able to do all things through the one who strengthens me." If taken without considering the context, this verse could be misinterpreted as being able to do whatever we desire, including hitting a home run, dunking a basketball, or winning the lottery. This particular verse is often misconstrued as a promise for such things. To properly understand what Paul said, we must consider the context in which Paul said it. Philippians 4:11-12 says:

> I am not saying this because I am in need, for I have learned to be content in any circumstance. I have experienced times of need and times of abundance. In any and every circumstance I have learned the secret of contentment, whether I go satisfied or hungry, have plenty or nothing.

It is incorrect to interpret this passage as a blank check, as if we can do *anything* we want through Christ. Paul was not saying he could break out of prison, conquer the Roman army, or anything like that. He was emphasizing that, through Christ, he could be content in every situation—specifically, any economic situation, whether "well fed or hungry, whether living in plenty or in want." Certainly, this is true for us as well. We can experience the joy of the Lord in any situation. In fact, we are commanded to "Rejoice in the Lord" (Phil 4:4) and "in everything give thanks" (1 Thess 5:18). These are disciplines we must practice, which are only possible because of Christ.

Here are some tips to help with applying the contextual principle:

- Discover the immediate context of the surrounding verses or paragraph. This is done by reading the surrounding verses several times and asking questions like "What is the main thought or purpose of this section?"

- Discover the broader context of the chapter. Likewise, this is done by reading the chapter several times to discover the overarching theme. For example, the main theme in 1

Corinthians 12 is spiritual gifts. The main theme in 1 Corinthians 13 is love. The main theme in 1 Corinthians 14 is order in the church—specifically dealing with tongues and prophecy. The main theme in 1 Corinthians 15 is the resurrection. Some chapter themes are more challenging to discern, but knowing the chapter theme will help guide interpretation.

- Discover the overall context of the book. Again, after reading the book, ask questions like "Why was the book written?" or "What are the major theme(s) of the book?" "Are there any theme verses which clearly show the author's intent (cf. John 20:31, 1 Tim 3:14-15, 1 John 5:13)?" The answers to these questions can often be more quickly discovered in the introduction of a study Bible, Bible survey book, or commentary.

As the context of the surrounding verses, chapter, and book are identified, it will help guide and protect one's interpretation.

4. The Compatibility Principle

The best commentary on the Bible is the Bible itself. We must always interpret Scripture by comparing it to Scripture itself. If we come to an interpretation of a certain text that contradicts what the Bible says as a whole, then that interpretation must be wrong.

A great example of using the compatibility principle is seen in how Christ corrects Satan's abuse of Scripture when he tempted Christ in the wilderness. After Satan took Christ to the top of the temple, he said:

> … "If you are the Son of God, throw yourself down. For it is written, 'He will command his angels concerning you'

and 'with their hands they will lift you up, so that you will not strike your foot against a stone.'
Matthew 4:6

Satan interpreted Psalm 91:11-12 as a promise of God's protection in every situation, including a person intentionally trying to hurt himself. Essentially, Satan said to Christ, "Jump off this building because God has promised to protect you!" Psalm 91 certainly describes the blessings on the person who "lives in the shelter of the sovereign one" (v. 1) and makes his "refuge in the Lord" (v. 9); God often protects them in special ways. However, the Psalm does not tell the follower of the Lord to intentionally try to hurt himself. Christ corrects this misinterpretation, not by appealing to the immediate context of the Psalm, but by comparing Satan's interpretation to what Moses taught in Deuteronomy 6:16. In Matthew 4:7, Christ said, "Once again it is written: 'You are not to put the Lord your God to the test.'" Christ used the compatibility principle to prove Satan was twisting Psalm 91. We must do the same, both to find out what a verse means and what it does not mean.

The compatibility principle is especially important when considering what appears to be contradictory texts or doctrines. Here are a few rules to help with using the compatibility principle:

- **Rule 1:** *Use clear passages to interpret less-clear passages.* For example, 1 Corinthians 15:29 says, "Otherwise, what will those do who are baptized for the dead? If the dead are not raised at all, then why are they baptized for them?" What does "baptized for the dead" mean? Mormons have interpreted this to mean that one can be baptized in place of a dead person, thereby fulfilling the dead person's requirements for salvation. Whatever "baptized for the dead" means, it cannot mean that baptism saves anybody, whether they are dead or alive. This would

78

contradict the compatibility principle. Scripture clearly teaches that people are saved by faith and not works, including baptism (cf. Eph 2:8-9, John 3:16). Also, Scripture does not teach that our works or faith can save others. First Corinthians 15:29 is difficult to interpret and the compatibility principle helps protect us from error.

One possible explanation for this unclear passage is that Paul was referring to a pagan cult who lived just north of Corinth in a city called Eleusis, who practiced baptisms for the dead.[iii] That is why Paul said why are 'they'—not 'we'— baptized for 'them.' Since some were questioning the resurrection, Paul might have been saying, "Even pagans believe in the resurrection! Why are they baptizing people for the dead just north of Corinth?" as a challenge to the Corinthians' lack of belief. To properly interpret this unclear passage, both the compatibility principle and the historical principle (what was happening historically in and around Corinth) are needed. When encountering an unclear passage, consider what the Bible clearly teaches to help with interpreting the unclear.

- **Rule 2:** *Remember the Bible cannot contradict itself since God is its author and he cannot lie* (cf. Titus 1:2). Scripture, in its original manuscripts, is without error. If two passages contradict one another, this means our interpretation of those passages is incorrect (possibly from not understanding the historical or literary context) or the translation of those passages is incorrect (possibly from wrongly translating the original language or even an error in the ancient manuscript used).

To successfully compare Scripture with Scripture, analyzing the cross-referenced verses in a study Bible, looking up key words in a Bible concordance to find similar verses, or studying a corresponding doctrine in a systematic theology or Bible encyclopedia are helpful.

5. The Grammatical Principle

The grammatical principle is simply recognizing rules of language, which include grammar and sentence structure. One must be able to recognize the subject and verb of a sentence—whether the verbs are past, present, or future tense. One should recognize when nouns or pronouns are singular, plural, possessive, or non-possessive. One should recognize adjectives, adverbs, dependent and independent clauses. It is particularly important to recognize conjunctions, as they connect words, sentences, phrases, and clauses. We will consider a few of them:

- "Therefore" instructs the reader to look back at what was previously talked about (a topic, verses, or even chapters) to properly understand what follows. It has often been said, "When you see the conjunction 'therefore,' you must look back to see what it is there for." For example, Hebrews 12:1 says: "Therefore, since we are surrounded by such a great cloud of witnesses, we must get rid of every weight and the sin that clings so closely, and run with endurance the race set out for us." The conjunction "therefore" points the reader back to Hebrews 11, the Heroes of the Faith chapter. The author is telling the reader that the great faith of these Old Testament heroes should inspire us to be faithful in our own spiritual journeys.

- "And" simply means "in addition to."

- "But" or "however" provides a contrast with what was previously said.

- "That," "then," "for," "so," and "because" are used to introduce a purpose or reason. For example, Romans 12:2 says, "Do not be conformed to this present world, but be transformed by the renewing of your mind, so that you may test and approve what is the will of God—what is good and well-pleasing and perfect." This verse hinges on the conjunction "so that." "So that" tells us that if we do not conform to the world but instead renew our mind, we grow in our ability to discern God's will. Consequently, those who are living in sin and not living in God's Word have problems discerning God's will for their lives and others. If we don't recognize the conjunction "so that," we will miss the logical flow of the author's statement.

- "If" provides a condition.

Without recognizing the grammar in a sentence, paragraph, or chapter, it is impossible to truly understand the meaning.

6. The Genre Principle

Since the Bible is a work of literature, it includes different literary styles called genres. To interpret verses in various genres, we must understand each genre's unique rules of interpretation. Thinking of the various genres as sports with different rules is helpful. For instance, in basketball, a person can't kick the ball like in soccer. And in soccer, one can't tackle like in football. Each game has its own rules; if those rules are broken, one will get a foul and possibly be removed from the game. Likewise, each genre has rules we must abide by to properly interpret a text. The primary genres are as follows:

- *Psalms* are poetic Hebrew prayers and songs. Since psalms are poetry, they use figures of speech, symbolism, and parallelism. A common feature of Hebrew parallelism is stating something in two ways: In synonymous parallelism, the author says one thing and then repeats it with different words. For example, Psalm 50:1 says, "Have mercy on me, O God, because of your loyal love! Because of your great compassion, wipe away my rebellious acts!" In antithetical parallelism, the second line provides a contrast with the first. For example, Psalm 1:6 says, "Certainly the Lord guards the way of the godly, but the way of the wicked ends in destruction."

- *Proverbs* are wise sayings about godly living presented in a short, memorable format. They should not be taken as promises but rather as general truths or common realities. For example, Proverbs 12:11 says, "The one who works his field will have plenty of food, but whoever chases daydreams lacks wisdom." In general, the person who works will have plenty of food, but this is not always true, for a variety of reasons (famine or drought, for example). Like the Psalms, the Proverbs often include figures of speech, symbolism, and parallelism.

- *Prophecy*, as a genre, includes God's speaking through prophets in both a foretelling and forthtelling fashion. Foretelling includes telling the future—speaking about the coming of the messiah, judgment, the day of the Lord, etc. Forthtelling is simply applying Scripture prophetically to God's people. Often the prophets shared how Israel broke God's law and called them to repentance. Most prophecy is forthtelling, not foretelling. A subgenre of prophecy is apocalyptic literature, which focuses on the end of the world by using symbols. Daniel, Ezekiel, and Revelation are prophetic/apocalyptic in nature.

- *History* tells the stories of the Bible. They detail redemptive history—how God brings about salvation through the messiah. They are descriptive in nature—showing us what happened—not prescriptive—showing us what to do. Throughout biblical history, we encounter the use of both negative and positive examples that warn and encourage us in our faith (1 Cor 10:6-11, Heb 12:1-3).

- *Parables* are symbolic stories with a spiritual meaning. It's important to remember that parables typically have one major point; therefore, significant meaning should not be applied to every detail of parables.

- *Epistles* teach us Christian doctrine, as written by the apostles and their associates.

It is important to identify the genre of specific writings so we can properly interpret them. Again, history is primarily meant to show us what happened, not to develop doctrines from. Throughout history, cults have taken the stories of polygamy (having multiple wives) in the Old Testament and made doctrines out of them—meaning they start to believe it is acceptable for men to have multiples wives. The narratives weren't meant for developing doctrines—that's what the epistles are for and the doctrinal aspects of the narratives, such as Christ's teachings in the Gospels. Similarly, with wisdom literature such as the Proverbs, if we make them promises, we will misinterpret and misapply them. They are simply general principles for wise living.

7. The Progressive Revelation Principle

God did not reveal all his truths at once. There is a continual progression of revelation throughout Scripture. To properly interpret, we must take into account the then-current state of revelation. We must ask, "What had God revealed to those people during that historical period?" When considering God's rejection of Cain's offering, it would be wrong to read into the narrative a full-blown understanding of the Mosaic law and its stipulations for offerings. At the time it happened, God hadn't made those known yet. Similarly, when reading the stories of Job and the Patriarchs, we must remember that no Scripture had yet been written, though God had certainly been speaking to them. Understanding how the original readers would perceive something is foundational for proper interpretation. Again, it is wrong to accept an interpretation of Scripture that the original audience would not have understood. This is only acceptable when later biblical authors reveal a deeper biblical meaning of a certain OT passage. For example, in John 3:14, Christ taught that when Moses instructed the dying Israelites to look at the bronze serpent to be healed, the bronze serpent was an Old Testament typology representing Christ. Christ would one day be put on a cross and those who looked to and believed in him would be saved. Though the original audience of Israelites wouldn't have understood that the bronze serpent had a deeper meaning, the Gospel of John tells us it does. As a general principle, we should not accept an interpretation that the original audience would not have naturally come to.

8. The Christological Principle

Christ is the major theme of Scripture, and therefore we should look for references to him throughout it and come to know him in a deeper way through our study. In John 5:39-40 and 46, Christ said this to unbelieving Jews:

You study the scriptures thoroughly because you think in them you possess eternal life, and it is these same scriptures that testify about me, but you are not willing to come to me so that you may have life. ... If you believed Moses, you would believe me, because he wrote about me.

Similarly, Jesus said this to his disciples after his resurrection, "These are my words that I spoke to you while I was still with you, that everything written about me in the law of Moses and the prophets and the psalms must be fulfilled" (Lk 24:44). The law of Moses, the Prophets, and the Psalms were one of the ways the ancient Jews referred to the whole Old Testament. All the Old Testament pointed to and was fulfilled in Christ.

In what ways is Christ seen throughout the whole Old Testament? (1) Christ is seen in prophetic references—prophecies about his birth, life, death, resurrection, and future reign. (2) He is seen in typologies—images of Christ throughout the Old Testament. Colossians 2:16-17 says, "Therefore do not let anyone judge you with respect to food or drink, or in the matter of a feast, new moon, or Sabbath days—these are only the shadow of the things to come, but the reality is Christ!" New Testament authors often alert us to OT pictures of Christ. Adam was a type of Christ (cf. Rom 5:14-15, 1 Cor 15:45). As Adam led the world into sin, Christ leads the world into righteousness. Moses was a type of Christ (cf. Dt 18:18, Acts 3:22). As Moses instituted the Old Covenant, Christ instituted the New Covenant. As mentioned, the bronze snake in the wilderness was a type of Christ (John 3:14). When the dying Israelites looked to the bronze snake on a pole for healing, it was a foreshadowing of how the world would look to Christ, who died on the cross, for salvation. (3) We also see Christ in the Old Testament law, not just in types, but also in the fact that the law ultimately demonstrated people's need for a savior. Galatians 3:24 says, "Thus the law had become our guardian [or

85

tutor] until Christ, so that we could be declared righteous by faith."
By giving the law to Israel, God taught them their inability to keep
God's law and that ultimate salvation could only come through the
prophesied messiah. (4) In addition, genealogies often point to
Christ. Many of them include members of Christ's lineage, as
demonstrated in his genealogical records in Matthew 1 and Luke
3.

However, not only is Christ promised in the Old Testament,
he is revealed throughout the New Testament. The four Gospels
tell his story. Acts details the building of his church through his
disciples. The Epistles share his teaching through the apostles.
Revelation teaches about his return, including his wrath, victory,
and kingdom.

The Christological principle does not mean we should
allegorize Scripture (making every detail a symbol of him) or think
that every verse directly points to Christ in some way. What it does
mean is that while studying Scripture, we should be aware that
there are often references to Christ throughout and take note of
them. Studying Scripture should make us know and love Christ
more.

9. The Church Witness Principle

Jesus taught that his sheep hear his voice and that they
would not follow the voice of another (John 10:4-8, cf. 1 John 2:20).
God has uniquely gifted his followers with the ability to understand
his Word. Second Corinthians 2:12 says we have received God's
Spirit "so that we may know the things that are freely given to us by
God." In addition, God has given gifted teachers to the church to
help believers come to a unity of the faith (Eph 4:14). Therefore, in
interpreting Scripture, there is great wisdom in finding out how
believers (present and past) have interpreted certain passages or
looked at certain doctrines. Proverbs 24:6 says, "for with guidance

you wage your war, and with numerous advisers there is victory." "Victory" can also be translated as "safety" (KJV).

We get a picture of this in Acts 15. There were false teachers in the early church, insisting that Gentiles needed to be circumcised and practice the Mosaic law (v. 1, 5). In response to this, Paul and Barnabas traveled from Antioch to Jerusalem to meet with the leaders of the church. After discussion, James, the leader of the Jerusalem church, definitively declared that Gentiles did not have to be circumcised, nor practice the Mosaic law (v. 19-20).

Similarly, there has been significant attacks on specific doctrines throughout history, causing the church to bond together and wrestle with Scripture to discern what it truly says—often leading to a general consensus. For instance, the doctrine of the Trinity, the full deity and humanity of Christ, and the inerrancy of Scripture, have all been grappled with and agreed upon by the majority of the church throughout history. There is great wisdom and protection in studying the conclusions of the ancient and contemporary church.

With that said, simply because the majority of the church believes something (or has believed something), doesn't necessarily mean it's correct. It does mean that we should give great consideration to their conclusion. This is where cults have often failed. Though the church has largely accepted the doctrine of the Trinity, the deity/humanity of Christ, or salvation by faith alone, cults choose to ignore those conclusions—believing that God has given them special revelation that the majority of the church has missed. As Scripture tells us, there is safety and victory in the multitude of counselors. Christ has uniquely given his church the ability to understand his Word; therefore, we must consider the historical conclusions of other saints. This can be done by studying commentaries and systematic theologies, both contemporary and ancient ones.

What are some tips for applying the church witness principle?

- *We must be humble.* Pride often leads to false interpretation, but a wise person is humble and seeks the insight of others.

- *We must be resourceful.* It often takes hard work and diligent study to research problem passages or doctrines; however, there is great fruit in such efforts.

- *We must, at times, be willing to break from the majority or from what is familiar to us.* Just because the majority agrees on some point, or because we were raised in a denomination or church that believes a certain doctrine, doesn't mean either is right. Throughout history, there have been seasons where the majority fell into serious Scriptural error, and certainly no church, denomination, or individual is immune to this. We must recognize this and therefore be committed to God's Word more than a denomination, church, or individual.

Conclusion

What are some hermeneutical principles to help us properly interpret Scripture?

1. **The Literal Principle**. We should read Scripture according to its plain sense. If the plain sense makes good sense, seek no other sense, lest we make nonsense.

2. **The Historical Principle**. We must understand the historical background including the author, audience, ancient culture, and setting, to properly interpret.

3. **The Contextual Principle**. We must consider the literary context of the surrounding verses, the chapter, and ultimately the book in which a verse is found to properly interpret. Without context, a verse can mean anything.

4. **The Compatibility Principle**. Since Scripture is the best commentary on Scripture, we must consider a verse in comparison to what the rest of Scripture says. Scripture cannot contradict itself, and we should use clear verses to interpret less clear ones.

5. **The Grammatical Principle**. We must recognize and understand proper grammar including sentence structure to properly interpret.

6. **The Genre Principle**. Each genre has different rules, and if we do not follow them, our interpretations will be inaccurate. A proverb is not a promise; it is a general principle. We should not add significance to every detail of a parable. Historical narratives are descriptive, not necessarily prescriptive.

7. **The Progressive Revelation Principle**. Understanding how the original audience would comprehend a verse is crucial to interpretation; therefore, we must recognize the revelation that the original audience had.

8. **The Christological Principle**. Christ is the major theme of Scripture. The Old Testament points to him, and the New Testament is the fulfillment. As we study, we should recognize references to him and seek to know Christ more through our study.

9. **The Church Witness Principle**. How has the church throughout history understood a certain text or doctrine? This will often help us properly understand a text and protect us from grievous errors, which people often repeat.

Reflection

1. In the reading, what principle stood out most to you and why?
2. What are some good tips for applying the literary contextual principle?
3. What are some of the different genres in Scripture and rules for properly interpreting them?
4. In what ways does all of Scripture point to Christ?
5. How can we apply the church witness principle when studying difficult passages or doctrines?
6. In what ways have cults commonly rejected the church witness principle throughout history?
7. What other questions or applications do you have from the reading?

Life Application

There is a story of a young man who was looking for direction in life. "What should I do with my life?" he prayed. He opened his Bible and put his finger in it—hoping that God would give him direction. It landed on Matthew 27:5, which read, "Then he went out and hanged himself." Perplexed, not understanding what the text meant for his life, he tried again. This time his finger landed in Luke 10:37, which read, "So Jesus said to him, 'Go and do the same.'" Becoming nervous, he tried one more time, with his finger landing in John 13:27. It read, "Jesus said to him, 'What you are about to do, do quickly.'" Though humorous, this story illustrates the dangerous ways in which some people are tempted to apply Scripture.

What are some principles that will help with applying Scripture? For both laymen and serious Bible students, application is often the hardest part of Bible study. Many people have left their devotions or a sermon struggling with the question, "What do I do with what I've learned?" Application is the "so what" after understanding what a passage means. It is taking a passage originally written to an ancient world and applying it in the contemporary world. In this lesson, we will consider principles that help with proper application.

Recognize the Dispensation

Throughout history, there have been appalling misapplications of Scripture, such as with early Americans burning witches during the Salem Witch Trials, or the enslavement of Africans. These tragic errors often happen, in part because when studying the Bible, people don't recognize the different dispensations in Scripture and therefore misapply the texts. It has often been said, "Everything written in the Bible is written for us, but everything written is not necessarily written to us." This is why recognizing dispensations, or epochs of biblical history, is so important.

Recognizing dispensations essentially means asking the question, "Am I part of the people to whom this portion of Scripture was originally written?" For example, Israel was originally called to practice the Sabbath by not working from Friday sundown until Saturday sundown. Those who broke this law were to be stoned (Num 15:32-36). Since Paul taught that we are not under the Old Covenant but under the New Covenant (cf. Rom 6:14), we as Christians don't practice this regulation, and we certainly don't stone anybody. In addition, the necessity of practicing certain dietary restrictions and festivals given to Israel were removed in the New Covenant (Col 2:16-17).

Recognizing dispensations is also important when considering prophetic literature. For instance, in Revelation 13, the Antichrist and his prophet command people to accept the mark of the beast, and those who won't, cannot buy or sell. One must ask, "Has this prophecy been fulfilled or is it still anticipating future fulfillment?" If this passage awaits a later fulfillment, it would be wrong to directly apply this to people in the current dispensation by saying something like: "Do not accept _____ or you will have accepted the mark of the beast and therefore are under God's judgment!" In addition, there are prophecies that only fit in the millennial kingdom—such as people living extraordinarily long lives during that period, and those who die before 100 years of age being considered accursed (Is 65:20). Again, since this passage awaits a later fulfillment, it would be wrong to declare that somebody who currently doesn't live to 100 is cursed by God. To apply those promises to this age would be to misapply them. Recognizing dispensations is important for proper application.

If we are going to recognize dispensations, we must first ask, "What is a dispensation?" Dispensations are periods of time or stages in biblical history where God has given particular moral responsibilities to his people. A dispensation is often marked by:

- the giving of certain responsibilities
- a specific time period these responsibilities last
- the end of previous responsibilities
- the continuation of other responsibilities

What are some questions for us to ask in order to discern the dispensation of a passage?

✓ Who was the passage originally written to or intended for (Israel, the church, people during the tribulation, etc.)?

✓ Are the principles taught in this passage timeless, or do they apply only to the original audience or a specific future audience (such as with end time prophecy)?

✓ If the passage is prophetic, has the prophecy already been fulfilled?

What are the dispensation periods in the Bible and the regulations given in them? Below is a brief summary of commonly recognized periods:

1. *Innocence* (from the creation of man to the fall of man). Adam and Eve were called to tend the garden and to be fruitful and multiply. They were called to eat only plant life. The only clear prohibition given was to not eat of the tree of good and evil. This dispensation ended in Genesis 3, when man ate of the forbidden tree and sin entered the world.

2. *Conscience* (from the fall to the flood). God did not give rules to humanity during this time. Scripture records no "thou shalts!" or "thou shalt nots!" Humanity was ruled by their God-given moral conscience, which they clearly rejected (cf. Rom 2:14-15). Genesis 6:5 says, "But the LORD saw that the wickedness of humankind had become great on the earth. Every inclination of the thoughts of their minds was only evil all the time."

3. *Human Government* (from after the flood). After the flood, God established capital punishment for the death of a human, whether the murder was committed by another person or an animal (Gen 9:2-6). This represented the establishment of civil government. God told Noah that whoever shed the blood of man by man, his blood would be shed. In addition, God said that both plants and animals would be food for humans.

4. *Promise* (from the patriarchs). God chose to make a covenant with Abraham and his seed to bless the world (cf. Gen 12:1-3, 22:15-18, Gal 3:7). This was fulfilled in Israel, who became the stewards of God's law and the temple. It was ultimately fulfilled through the promised Jewish messiah—Jesus Christ—who has truly blessed the world by providing a means of reconciliation with God through his death for sin and resurrection. This promise will be fulfilled completely when Christ returns and rules on the earth.

5. *The Mosaic Law* (from Mount Sinai to the cross). This covenant was established with Israel on Mount Sinai with the Ten Commandments and the law. God called Israel to be a priestly nation that would bless the world. Israel was required to obey the Mosaic law. If they did, God would bless them, and if they did not, God would curse them (Dt 28). The Mosaic law was perfectly fulfilled through Christ's righteous life and death for sin, which paid the penalty for everyone's sins (cf. Matt 5:17, Rom 10:4). The

Mosaic law was temporary and ended upon Christ's death (cf. 2 Cor 3:7-11).

6. *Church* (from Pentecost to the Rapture/Second Coming). In Acts 2, at Pentecost, the promised Holy Spirit came upon the church—baptizing her, making her the body of Christ, and empowering her to serve the Lord (1 Cor 12:13). The church is a gathering of believers, Jewish and Gentile, together in one body. In Ephesians 3:4-6, Paul called this a mystery which was not fully revealed to past generations. This age will be marked by the gospel going out to the nations. It will continue until Christ raptures his church, giving each member a resurrected body.

(6b.) *Tribulation* (from the final years of the Church Age to the Second Coming or from Rapture to Second Coming). Historically, most believe that the church age will last until Christ comes, which would include the church going through the tribulation period. In the tribulation, Satan will deceive the nations through the Antichrist, and God will pour out his judgment on the nations (Rev 5-19). Then Christ will come, rapture his church, and judge the nations. This is called the historical premillennial view. However, one of the most popular views today is the premillennial dispensational view. They believe that the church age will end at the rapture, when Christ secretly comes to take his church to heaven before (or during) the seven-year tribulation. The tribulation will end when Christ visibly and triumphantly returns with his saints to rule and judge the earth.

7. *The Messianic Kingdom* (from the Second Coming to the Great White Throne of Judgment). According to Revelation 20, when Christ returns, he will judge the world and Satan, and then establish a 1000-year rule of peace. After this time, Satan will be let loose to deceive the nations into rebelling against Christ. Christ will destroy the rebels, and then unbelievers will be resurrected for their final judgment at the Great White Throne of Judgment, after which they

will be cast into the lake of fire. Some interpret Revelation 20 as symbolically representing the church age, with Christ eventually coming to judge the world and Satan, and then ushering in the eternal stage. This is called the amillennial view.

8. *The Eternal Stage* (from the Renewal of the Heaven and Earth to Eternity). God will renew the heaven and earth through fire (2 Pt 3:10-13)—creating a new heaven and earth. The capital city of heaven, Jerusalem, will come to earth thereby making it heaven on earth. The nations of the earth will flock to Jerusalem, as God's presence will abide there. There will be no evil, mourning, or death in the new heaven and earth (Rev 21-22).

Again, recognizing the dispensation is important to properly apply Scripture. Everything is written for us but not everything was written to us. With that said, all Scripture has applications, but they are not always direct applications, such as Israel stoning those who didn't practice the Sabbath, or those living during the tribulation being warned about not accepting the mark of the beast, or, during the millennium age, those people who die before reaching 100 years of age being considered accursed. In those cases, we look for contemporary equivalents which correlate with the time frame we live in.

Find Contemporary Equivalents

The next thing we must do to apply a text is to find the contemporary equivalent. Keep in mind, there are varying degrees of contemporary equivalency, depending on the historical context. Sometimes the equivalency remains the same, as with truths like "do not lie, steal, or murder." However, with commands or maxims such as not eating food offered to idols or not muzzling an ox while it treads grain, it becomes more difficult to discern. When considering contemporary equivalency, the closer we are to the

97

same historical situation in the Scripture, the greater authority the application has. The further away, the less authority the application might have.

How can we find contemporary equivalents, especially when the ancient situations are so different? To help, here are some situations to identify and questions to ask:

Identify the People

Begin by identifying the people in the passage, the characters who are actively involved. Sometimes no specific individuals or groups will be named (such as when reading specific passages in Proverbs or Romans). Instead, focus on the author, the original audience, and God. Ask questions like:

✓ Who are the people in this passage?
✓ How are these people like people in my world or how do they represent situations in my world?
✓ What characteristics of these people do I see in myself or others?

Let's consider the story of David and Goliath. Who are the people in that story? They are David, Goliath, Saul, Israel, and the Philistines. Considering each character's role in the story will help with finding applications. For example, Israel (the people of God) might have applications for the church. Saul might have special applications for a spiritual or secular leader. The Philistines might have applications for the world and its ungodly influence. Goliath might have applications for a prideful person (or a difficult trial we encounter). David might have applications for any child of God. To whom do we relate most: the faithless Israelites, faithful David, the unbelieving and antagonistic Philistines, the scared leader, Saul, the proud giant, Goliath? How are the people in the story most similar to those around us? Identifying and considering the people is an important step towards application, especially when reading narratives.

Identify the Place

This step places the passage in its original setting—the historical and cultural context. The more one knows about the culture, history, and problems of the people in the passage, the more one will be able to find parallels to life today. Ask questions like:

- ✓ What is the setting of this passage?
- ✓ What are the significant details in the history, culture, and geography?
- ✓ What are the similarities to my world?

Is the context the Jews in the wilderness, as in parts of Exodus and the books of Numbers and Deuteronomy? Is the context the exiled Israelites serving in Babylon, as in Ezekiel or the book of Daniel? Understanding the context helps identify applications. For example, Israel's years of wandering in the wilderness might have general applications to going through trials and waiting seasons. The Israelites' being exiled in Babylon might have applications for working or going to school in a secular environment.

Identify the Plot

This step answers, "What's happening in the storyline?" Usually, this can be discovered by knowing the context of the passage or the book. Ask questions like:

- ✓ What is happening in this passage? Is it persecution, war, trials, or false teaching?
- ✓ What is the conflict or tension?
- ✓ What would I have done in this situation?
- ✓ How is this similar to what is happening in my life or in the world today?

For example, in the book of Judges, the storyline is the recurring unfaithfulness of the Israelites, God's discipline through hostile nations, Israel's repentance, God's deliverance through a judge, and the story repeating itself. As we consider the storyline in the book of Judges, we can apply this to ourselves personally, to our churches, and to our nations. We routinely repeat patterns of sin, discipline, repentance, and restoration. Israel's example should remind us to turn away from sin and remain faithful to God. It should also help us be prophets to others who persist in those patterns.

Identify the Main Theme (or Themes)

To do this, we should ask questions like:

- ✓ What was the message for the original audience?
- ✓ What were they supposed to learn?
- ✓ What did God want them to do?

Often, the theme of a book is clearly stated. For example, in 1 John 5:13, John says, "I have written these things to you who believe in the name of the Son of God so that you may know that you have eternal life." The major theme of the book is assurance of salvation—knowing that one has eternal life. Throughout the book, John provides tests of true salvation, which have very direct applications to Christians today. In other books, the theme is discerned by its repetition throughout the book. For example, in Philippians, the words "joy" and "rejoice" are used more than twelve times.[iv] Therefore, having joy in the Lord is one of the main themes of the book. This theme stands out even more when considering the historical context: Paul wrote the book, while he was in prison, to Christians who were suffering persecution. Certainly, this theme should challenge readers to pursue joy in the Lord regardless of their situation, even as Paul encouraged the Philippians to do so. Understanding the theme of a book is important for discerning applications.

Identify Universal Principles

When studying a text, we should always look for universal principles. For example, when Christ was tempted by the devil in the wilderness, he always countered with Scripture. Consider Matthew 4:3-4:

> The tempter came and said to him, "If you are the Son of God, command these stones to become bread." But he answered, "It is written, 'Man does not live by bread alone, but by every word that comes from the mouth of God.'

We must ask ourselves, "What are the universal truths in this passage?" In order to defeat temptation in our lives, we must know God's Word and directly apply it to specific temptations. If this is a timeless principle, we should be able to see it taught throughout Scripture, which we do. In Psalms 119:11, David said, "In my heart I store up your words, so I might not sin against you." By memorizing Scripture, David was able to defeat specific temptations. We also see support for this universal principle in Paul's call to take up the sword of the Spirit, the Word of God, to stand against Satan and demons (Eph 6:17). Each specific

Scripture is meant to help us defeat the devil in the specific way he attacks.

How do we find universal principles? We should ask questions like:

✓ What is the message for all mankind?
✓ What are the timeless truths?

To apply Scripture, we must identify the people, the place, the plot, the major themes of the ancient text, and find universal principles for our contemporary world.

Find General Principles by Broadening the Application of Specific Ones

For example, in 1 Corinthians 9:9 and 14, Paul said this:

For it is written in the law of Moses, "Do not muzzle an ox while it is treading out the grain."

God is not concerned here about oxen, is he? ... In the same way the Lord commanded those who proclaim the gospel to receive their living by the gospel.

"Do not muzzle an ox while it is treading out the grain" was originally written to Israel in the book of Deuteronomy. Israel was a farming society, to which that passage directly applied. How might we apply the truth in that passage to contemporary society? Consider how Paul applied it: in the same way that an ox should be able to eat from the grain that he is laboring over, pastors should be able to make their living from preaching the gospel. Although we are New Testament believers, and not under the rule of Old Testament law specifically addressed to Israel, applications and abiding truths can still be applied. The specific contemporary application to not muzzle an ox would be for farmers to provide food for their laboring animals. But the general principle presented here is that a laborer is worthy of his wages, which applies to pastors or any other laborer.

Here is a contemporary illustration: if a wife asks her husband to pick up his shoes, the direct or specific application would be for him to pick up the shoes. But what is the general application which the wife really wants (one that a wise, discerning husband will understand)? The general application is that the husband not create more work for her by making a mess, which applies to more than just leaving his shoes lying around. Also, the wife is probably implying, "Help out around the house, please!" When deriving meaning from conversations, we go from specific to general all the time. We're simply discerning the broader principle behind someone's words.

Find the Sin Principle

Bryan Chapell, the former President of Covenant Seminary, calls this the "Fallen Condition Focus." Since Scripture was written to sinners so they can become saved, and to believers so they can become holy (2 Tim 3:14-17), each text, whether explicitly or implicitly, exposes our spiritual brokenness. Consider the following texts:

> Every scripture is inspired by God and useful for teaching, for reproof, for correction, and for training in righteousness, that the person dedicated to God may be capable and equipped for every good work.
> 2 Timothy 3:16-17

These things happened to them as examples and were written down as warnings for us, on whom the fulfillment of the ages has come.
1 Corinthians 10:11

For everything that was written in former times was written for our instruction, so that through endurance and through encouragement of the scriptures we may have hope.
Romans 15:4

Through Scripture, God is pointing out people's sin and calling them to salvation and righteousness. Therefore, to properly apply Scripture, we must identify the sin principle behind the text. We should ask, "In what way is God exposing the spiritual brokenness of the original audience?"

Even passages that deal specifically with encouragement or grace in a sense still reckon with sin. For example, Philippians 4:4 says, "Rejoice in the Lord always. I will say it again: Rejoice!" What is the sin that the Holy Spirit is identifying through this passage? The sin is their propensity to lack divine joy and to live in discouragement—as though God were not in control, working things for their good—and also how they probably sought joy in things other than God, which left them empty. Certainly, circumstances affected this: they were being persecuted (Phil 1:27), they had false teaching in the church (Phil 2:2), and they had discord (Phil 4:2); however, they could still have joy in Christ, regardless of their circumstances. Like the Philippians, we often lack joy in the Lord and often fail to seek it from him. We try to find our joy in other things, things that can never satisfy. This is what the Holy Spirit was seeking to expose and change in the original audience and in our lives.

Let's consider another passage: What is the sin principle in Romans 12:2? It says, "Do not be conformed to this present world, but be transformed by the renewing of your mind, so that you

104

may test and approve what is the will of God—what is good and well-pleasing and perfect."

The primary issue that the Holy Spirit seems to be addressing was the Roman Christians' tendency to model the world and think like them. This is true of believers throughout history. Israel wanted to be like the ungodly nations: to be ruled by a king, worship idols, and practice their sexual ethics (or lack of). Similarly, contemporary Christians often look just like the world in their entertainment, language, dress, and ethics.

As we have seen, the sin principle is often clear in warning passages (like "do not conform to the world") but it is also implicit within grace-filled passages. Philippians 4:13 says, "I am able to do all things through the one who strengthens me." Implied in this verse is the fact that we often lack the ability to do what God has called us to do because we rely on our own strength instead of God's. Paul was able to be faithful in prosperity or poverty because of Christ (cf. Phil 4:10-11), and the Philippians could find grace in their own circumstances through Christ as well. The sin principle is the believers' tendency to not rely on Christ, but instead strive to do things through their own power.

How can we find the sin principle in any given Bible passage?

✓ Identify a key word which points out or implies sin.

In Romans 12:2, "Do not conform to the pattern of this world," the key word is "conform." The believers were conforming to the world. In Philippians 4:4, "Rejoice in the Lord! Again, I say rejoice!" The key word is "rejoice." It implies a sin problem: a lack of joy in the Lord, or a lack of seeking joy in the Lord. In Philippians 4:13, "I can do all this through him who gives me strength," the key word is "strength." Because we don't rely on God but instead seek to do things in our own power, we are often weak and discouraged. In the last two examples (Phil 4:4 and 4:13), the sin was implicit, not explicit; therefore, we simply considered the opposite of the key words. The opposite of "rejoicing" in the Lord is having a lack of joy from not abiding in Christ. The opposite of "strength" which comes from the Lord is weakness which comes from a lack of abiding in him. An implied sin can often be identified by considering the opposite of the key word.

Another example of this is Colossians 3:16, which says, "Let the word of Christ dwell in you richly, teaching and exhorting one another with all wisdom, singing psalms, hymns, and spiritual songs, all with grace in your hearts to God." The key word is "dwell." In Greek, it means to "dwell as a resident." Though this is not a warning passage, it implies that God's Word is often more like a visitor in many believers' lives rather than a resident. Because of this, they don't experience the blessings of God's Word indwelling them, such as teaching others with wisdom, singing to the Lord, and being thankful. The sin principle in Colossians 3:16 is the believers' tendency to not dwell in God's Word and how they, therefore, lack the corresponding fruits.

✓ Remember that the original audience had sin that needed to be remedied, whether it was unbelief, worldliness, pride, or willful rebellion, and so do we.

Some people only see the sin of others in Scripture and not the sin in their own lives. It's like those who listen to sermons and think about how it applies to somebody else, without recognizing their own need for the message. Israel worshiped idols, but we have our own idols, even if they are our job, spouse, digital toys, clothes, or future plans, etc. To find the sin principle, we must remember that the Holy Spirit was trying to make the original audience holy in some specific way, as he is also doing in us. We must find that 'holy burden' in the text and apply it to our lives.

Find the Grace Principle

Just as there are underlying sin principles in every passage, often grace principles are present as well. Throughout all of Scripture, we encounter grace: evidences of God's care and unmerited favor toward humanity. After Adam and Eve sinned by not trusting God, God gave the promise of the messiah. After the flood, God gave the rainbow. When Israel was in sin, he sent prophets. After the crucifixion, there was the resurrection. There is often grace to be found within a text.

To accurately discern the grace principle, we need to consider the context of the whole story. For example, while God is not explicitly named in the book of Esther, his fingerprints are clearly identifiable. We can recognize God's sovereign hand in the unfolding events of the story. Was it mere coincidence, when the enemies of Israel had received permission to destroy the Jews, that the king was married to a Jewish woman and that her Jewish uncle had recently foiled a plot to kill the king? Certainly not. God providentially intervened to bring redemption for the Jews, as they were given permission by the king to destroy their enemies. Esther's story demonstrates how God defends his people and uses all things (including evil) for their good (cf. 2 Thess 3:3, Rom 8:28, Eph 1:11).

Let's consider Matthew 11:28-30 as another example:

Come to me, all you who are weary and burdened, and I will give you rest. Take my yoke on you and learn from me, because I am gentle and humble in heart, and you will find rest for your souls. For my yoke is easy to bear, and my load is not hard to carry.

In this text, the grace principle is Christ's promise to give rest. However, we must notice that this promise is conditional. Christ only bestows this grace upon those who come to him in salvation and serve with him ("take my yoke upon you"). Not everybody experiences Christ's rest and, of those who do, some experience it to greater degrees, as they faithfully serve with Christ in reaching the world.

What are some questions that will help us identify the grace principle?

✓ What is God doing in the text, in view of the audience?

✓ Is the promise or work of God conditional or unconditional? For example, "I will never leave you nor forsake you" (Heb 13:5) is unconditional. "Think on these things, put them into practice and the God of peace will be with you" (Phil 4:8-9 paraphrase) is conditional.

✓ How does it apply to me?

To apply, we should consider what God is doing in the text and if there are any promises that we should receive or pursue.

Understand Contemporary Culture (Cultural Exegesis)

Cultural exegesis is essentially being able to critically evaluate culture—understanding its norms, strengths, weaknesses, etc.—and apply Scripture to it. This is important so we can apply Scripture both to ourselves (as participants in a culture) and to the world around us.

Let's consider an example: James 5:16 says, "So confess your sins to one another and pray for one another so that you may be healed. The prayer of a righteous person has great effectiveness." If confessing our sins and praying for one another leads to healing, how does a people (and the culture they represent) fail to do this and miss God's promises? Since the fall, people have lived with shame, leading them to spiritually, emotionally, and physically try to hide from God and from others.

Unfortunately, this is true in our churches, as well. Many Christians lack open relationships with others, where they are confessing sin, praying for one another, and receiving God's healing. In some ethnic cultures, like Asian ones, the concept of "saving face" is exceedingly powerful; the cultural requirement to "save face" can hinder transparent sharing and the healing God promises. Recognizing tendencies of a particular culture are critical for discerning applications.

To practice cultural exegesis, we must ask questions like:

- ✓ What are the greatest strengths of this culture?
- ✓ What are the greatest weaknesses of this culture?
- ✓ What are the opportunities in this culture?

These questions should be applied to a nation, a city, an ethnic group, an age group, a gender, a family, and even ourselves.

One obstacle to doing cultural exegesis, and therefore applying the Bible to our lives and others, is that sometimes it's hard to identify strengths and weaknesses within our own culture. Often, we just accept norms of our cultural environment without questioning or weighing them against Scripture. However, to properly apply Scripture to ourselves and others, we must understand our own culture and the cultures of those God has called us to minister.

In 1 Corinthians 9:19-22, Paul said this:

> For since I am free from all I can make myself a slave to all, in order to gain even more people. To the Jews I became like a Jew to gain the Jews. To those under the law I became like one under the law (though I myself am not under the law) to gain those under the law. To those free from the law I became like one free from the law (though I am not free from God's law but under the law of

Christ) to gain those free from the law. To the weak I became weak in order to gain the weak. I have become all things to all people, so that by all means I may save some.

Essentially, Paul did cultural exegesis—learning a culture and adopting non-sinful aspects of it in order to win the people of that culture to Christ. We must learn to do the same in order to effectively apply God's Word to ourselves and those around us.

Develop an Action Plan

James 1:22 says, "But be sure you live out the message and do not merely listen to it and so deceive yourselves." If we are going to do what Scripture says, we must not only discern the application of Scripture, but also plan how to apply it. Proverbs 21:5 says, "The plans of the diligent lead only to plenty." It has also often been said, "To fail to plan is to plan to fail." Therefore, if we are going to apply Scripture, we must make an action plan.

What are some questions and steps to help develop an effective action plan? We should ask ourselves:

- ✓ What does God want me to do about what I have learned?
- ✓ What steps will get me to that goal?
- ✓ What should be my first step?
- ✓ Whom should I seek to pray for me and hold me accountable in this process?

These plans will be conditional or unconditional, depending on the passage and our status. For example, Ephesians 5:25-27 says:

Husbands, love your wives just as Christ loved the church and gave himself for her to sanctify her by cleansing her with the washing of the water by the word, so that he may present the church to himself as glorious—not having a stain or wrinkle, or any such blemish, but holy and blameless.

For the husband who wants to love his wife by washing her with the Word, an unconditional action plan might be:

1) Approach his wife about considering a daily time to read God's Word and pray together.
2) Ask spiritual leaders to recommend good devotional books to read with his wife.
3) Attend a good Bible-preaching church.
4) Ask a godly friend to hold him accountable in his seeking to be the spiritual leader of his family.

For a single woman hoping to eventually be married, she might have a conditional plan that starts with, "When considering a potential husband, I will look for a spiritual leader." For a single man, his conditional plan might start with, "I will focus on growing spiritually first before pursuing a potential wife."

The plans of the diligent lead to profit. If we're going to apply God's Word, we must make action plans—both conditional and unconditional ones.

Conclusion

What principles should one employ to find biblical applications?

1. **Recognize the Dispensation**. Consider the time period in biblical history, the audience, and if the text directly applies to the church.

2. **Find Contemporary Equivalents**. Consider the people, place, plot, and themes to find universal principles.
3. **Find General Principles by Broadening the Application of Specific Ones**. Learn to consider not only what is directly said but the implications of a matter.
4. **Find the Sin Principle**. Find out what aspect of our spiritual brokenness the Holy Spirit is seeking to reveal through the passage.
5. **Find the Grace Principle**. Find out how God is moving in the text and how he is asking us to trust him.
6. **Understand Contemporary Culture (Cultural Exegesis)**. Think not only about the ancient world but the contemporary world as well, noting its strengths and weaknesses, and how Scripture speaks to these traits.
7. **Develop an Action Plan**. It is not enough to figure out an application; we must consider practically how to implement it and then follow through.

Reflection

1. In the reading, what principle stood out most to you and why?
2. What does the statement, "Everything was written for us but not to us," mean?
3. What are the sin principle and the grace principle in Scripture? Are both always in the text? Why or why not?
4. Why is doing cultural exegesis important? How can we practice cultural exegesis in our families, workplaces, cities, or nations?
5. Why is it important to not only find Scriptural applications but also to make action plans after?
6. What other questions or applications do you have from the reading?

Bible Study Methods

When people go to the gym and work out, they often don't see results for at least two reasons: For some, they do the same exercises over and over again. Our bodies adapt really well to repeated actions, and therefore, our muscles stop growing in endurance, strength, and size. For others, they simply have no plan at all. They aimlessly pick up this weight or work out on that equipment. Without any real plan, they don't see much positive change. Both groups often become bored and discouraged with their workouts, in part for lack of results.

People often experience this in their Bible study times as well—going through seasons of dryness—not as interested, motivated, or fruitful. Sometimes this happens because of unrepentant sin in their lives, but often it is like people in the gym—they have no Bible study method at all (just picking random chapters and verses), or they do the same thing over and over again and have never changed. Often using a different Bible study method brings freshness to our study of Scripture—inspiring us and making our time more fruitful.

There are many Bible study methods, each with different aims and benefits. To have a balanced method of study, we need to both study the breadth of Scripture—seeing the big picture—and the depth of Scripture—seeing the details in every book, chapter, and verse. All methods have their benefits, and so it is wise to at times employ various ones. We'll consider several different methods that can enhance our understanding and enjoyment of studying the Bible.

The Read the Entire Bible Method

The "read the entire Bible method" is just that: one reads the Bible completely every couple of months, once a year, or once every couple of years. It is important to read the entire Bible multiple times so one can understand the whole and how it relates to the parts. Without routinely doing this, one will be more prone to misinterpret and misapply Scripture. The Bible, though comprised of individual books, is a whole and must be understood as a whole.

How much time should it take one to read the entire Bible? Various Bible reading plans can be found, many of them on the Internet. In general, a person can read the Bible completely in a year if he or she reads 3.25 chapters per day (or, around twelve to fifteen minutes a day). Also, a person can read the Bible every three months by reading thirteen chapters a day (around fifty to sixty minutes per day). This could be done by having two thirty-minute Bible reading sessions a day, perhaps in the morning and in the evening.

We've considered the amount of time required; now let's consider how one should read strategically through the Bible books. Again, there are many plans. Most people initially try to read straight through from Genesis to Revelation. However, though zealous at the outset, they often get stuck in the wilderness of a few hard books (like Numbers and Leviticus) and don't pick it up again. To offset that possibility, many have found it helpful to read the Old Testament and New Testament concurrently—possibly a few chapters of the NT in the morning and a few of the OT at night. With that method, a person will repeat the New Testament, which has only twenty-seven books, several times, while simultaneously completing the Old Testament once, which has thirty-nine books.

The Expositional Method

The expositional method requires that one study a single Bible book deeply, to understand both the big picture and the details of the book, including verse meanings and applications. The word "exposition" simply means to "expose." A good example of this method is found in the book of Nehemiah, when the Levites read the Book of Law to the Israelites and then explained it to them. Nehemiah 8:7-8 says:

> Jeshua, Bani, Sherebiah, Jamin, Akkub, Shabbethai, Hodiah, Maaseiah, Kelita, Azariah, Jozabad, Hanan, and Pelaiah—all of whom were Levites—were teaching the people the law, as the people remained standing. They read from the book of God's law, explaining it and imparting insight. Thus the people gained understanding from what was read.

Exposition is more than simply reading the words on a page. It is purposeful reading with the intent of finding the meaning and application of the whole book, including understanding verses in their context.

How should one study a book expositionally? (1) Choose a book of the Bible to study. (2) Before beginning to study it, read the introductory material about the book in a study Bible or commentary. This will help a person see the forest before the trees—the big picture before the details. (3) Read a portion of the book: a paragraph, half a chapter, or a whole chapter. Probably an entire chapter is ideal. (4) Apply the OIL skills (Observation, Interpretation, and Life Application) while reading—noting details, asking questions, performing research to answer the questions, and finding applications. (5) Read a commentary or expositional sermon series alongside one's Bible reading to aid with understanding and application. A trustworthy free online resource is David Guzik's *Enduring Word Commentary*. (6) Complete an entire book of the Bible this way—verse by verse, section by section, chapter by chapter. Then, tackle another Bible book.

The Topical Method

A topical study is the study of a specific theme or subject in the Bible, such as the names of God, the characteristics of God, prayer, or spiritual disciplines. A great illustration of this method is when the resurrected Christ approached the disciples on their way to Emmaus. The disciples were discouraged because the messiah had died, and they were confused. Jesus encouraged them by guiding them through a topical study about the messiah through the Old Testament. In Luke 24:25-27, he said this:

> So he said to them, "You foolish people—how slow of heart to believe all that the prophets have spoken! Wasn't it necessary for the Christ to suffer these things and enter into his glory?" Then beginning with Moses and all the prophets, he interpreted to them the things written about himself in all the scriptures.

Christ took the disciples through the Old Testament passages, including prophecies and typologies, which showed how the messiah would die and enter into glory. For example, Isaiah 53 talks about how the messiah would be crushed for our iniquities, die, be buried, and be raised again. Psalm 16:10 (NIV) also describes how Christ, God's holy one, would not see decay. For the disciples to understand God's purpose in Christ's death and resurrection, they needed to know what Scripture specifically taught about those themes.

Similarly, we also gain great benefit from studying topics in Scripture. It starts with asking questions like, "What does the Bible teach about God's providence, spiritual disciplines, the church, creation, or the resurrection?"

How should we implement the topical study method? (1) Select a topic. (2) Use a concordance to look up relevant verses on that topic. (3) Study those verses by applying the OIL skills and consulting pertinent commentaries. (4) Finally, study books that have already thoroughly gathered and systemized Biblical information on those topics. Systematic theologies, Biblical encyclopedias, popular Christian books, and even websites like Bible.org or gotquestions.org, are helpful resources. For most, working backwards will be the best method to study a Bible topic. Gather books and articles that have systemized the biblical information on the topic (systematic theologies, articles, etc.). Then, study in detail the verses they cite. Just as Christ encouraged the disciples through this type of study, we'll often be greatly encouraged as well.

The Biographical Method

Another way that one can enrich his or her Bible study is by simply studying a Bible character. Researching that person's strengths, weaknesses, victories, failures, and life-changing experiences can provide insight into one's own life. Hebrews 12:1 says, "Therefore, since we are surrounded by such a great cloud of witnesses, we must get rid of every weight and the sin that clings so closely, and run with endurance the race set out for us." The "therefore" in the verse points the readers back to Chapter 11, which focuses on Old Testament heroes of the faith.

These Old Testament saints lived as pilgrims on earth as they awaited God's promises; they did mighty feats and suffered greatly, all while trusting in God. The author of Hebrews teaches us that contemplating the faith exhibited by these great saints helps us remove anything that hinders our spiritual journey, including sin, and inspires us to run our divinely given races with perseverance.

God specifically chose the Old Testament characters—including their failures and successes—to help us faithfully live our lives. Often, OT character studies are reserved only for children, but adults need to study them as well. In addition, there are also many New Testament characters to consider studying, such as the apostles and their associates.

How should one do a biographical study? (1) Study all the major passages covering the character's life. (2) Focus on the character's strengths, weaknesses, failures, successes, and impactful events. (3) Discern life principles that can be applied from their journey. (4) Read books or expositions that focus on the character's life.

Again, one can also work backwards by first studying the books that have systematized the biblical material, and using them to point to verses or experiences of the characters which can be studied in depth. Chuck Swindoll published a series called *Great Lives from God's Word*. Gene Getz wrote the series, *Men of Character*. John MacArthur published a book on the 12 disciples called *Twelve Ordinary Men*. *The Bible Teacher's Guide* has books on Abraham, Jacob, Joseph, and Nehemiah.

The Bible Memory Method

A commonly neglected method of studying the Bible is simply memorizing Scripture. In Psalm 119:11, David said, "In my heart I store up your words, so I might not sin against you." By memorizing Scripture, David found strength to conquer temptation. Similarly, when Christ was tempted by Satan in the wilderness, he continually contested each temptation with corresponding Scripture. Since Scripture is so important for prevailing against sin and temptation in the Christian life, it is very clear why so many succumb to temptation—they simply don't have God's Word hidden in them. They can't call upon it when encountering a lie of the enemy.

Bible memory is not easy. It takes dedication to memorize a verse and repetition to keep it memorized. However, the investment is worth it. It's important for victory in our own spiritual life and in helping others have victory. If a person memorizes one verse a month, that equals twelve a year, one verse every two weeks equals twenty-six a year, and one verse a week equals fifty-two a year.

The Meditation Method

This method is based on Psalm 1:2, where David described how God blessed the person who meditated on God's law, day and night. As mentioned, when considering how to develop Observation skills, the word "meditate" was used of a cow chewing its cud. Since the cow has a four-chambered stomach, it chews, digests to one chamber, regurgitates, chews again, digests to the second chamber, and so on. In this way, the cow extracts all the nutrients out of that one bite. Similarly, in the meditation method, a person reads one verse, or a couple of verses, over and over again, noting key words, repetitions, the context, the grammar, and other elements of the text, in order to understand, apply, and pray Scripture.

For example, one might read Psalm 23:1 (ESV) in the morning and meditate and pray on that for fifteen to thirty minutes. "The Lord is my Shepherd, I shall not want." The person would consider what it means for God to be "The Lord," what it means for God to be a "Shepherd," what it means for God to be "my" personal Shepherd, what it means to "want," what his or her "wants" are, and so on. Throughout the meditation, the person might write out questions, insights, applications, and prayer requests. The person may also read the verse in other Bible translations and read what commentaries say about it. They continually "chew" on the verse, talking to God about it and bringing requests before the Lord over it (for him or herself and also for others). Then, the next day, he or she would repeat the same process with Psalm 23:2.

This is the meditation method. One is trying to gain all the insight and nutrients possible from one verse or a few verses. When God's people do this and delight in it, God blesses them (Ps 1:1-3).

The Bible Mapping Method

In this method, a person will: (1) Choose a book of the Bible, for instance, Matthew. (2) Read Chapters 1-7 every day for seven days (or fewer chapters). (3) While reading each chapter, outline it, noting the major topic of the chapter, themes of paragraphs, flow, events, and significant verses. (4) Repeat this process with Chapters 8-14 for seven days, and so on. In four weeks, all twenty-eight chapters will be mapped out and the reader will have read Matthew seven times.

What's the benefit of this method? Many Christians can be called "concordance handicapped." They often say to themselves or others, "There is this verse… It says something like this… Where is it located?" By reading Matthew and outlining it seven times in a month, the map of each chapter will begin to stick in a person's mind. For example: In Matthew Chapter 1, we have Joseph's genealogy, Joseph being told about Mary's birth, and his marriage to her. In Chapter 2, we have the travels of the Magi to see Christ, Herod's anger and murder of innocent babies, and Joseph's family fleeing to Egypt. In Chapter 3, we have John the Baptist's ministry, which includes Jesus' baptism. Because of the repetition, a person's mind begins to store up and organize information and operate like a concordance.

There is great benefit in studying each book of the Bible this way. One's mind will develop a map of each Bible book and cease to be as dependent upon secondary resources (or other people) to navigate through the Bible.

The Devotional Method

This Bible study method is very popular. With it, Christians allow a devotional book to direct their Bible study. Each chapter of the devotional book focuses on a verse or verses to read, providing a devotional article that gives practical insights about that Bible passage and possibly a prayer that the reader can lift up to the Lord. The primary purpose of this method is not necessarily to gain a deeper Scriptural knowledge, but rather to find immediate encouragement and strength for the day. There are many popular devotional books. One of the most popular is Oswald Chambers' *My Utmost for His Highest*.

Though the devotional method is extremely popular, it should not be the only method used. It tends to make the reader more dependent upon the secondary resource (the devotional book), rather than the Bible. It is best used as a supplement to one's regular Bible study.

The Bible Survey Method

The purpose of the survey method is to gain a general understanding of every book of the Bible. Typically, one would read a Bible survey book that gives introductory material to every book of the Bible including: author, audience, date, historical background, major themes in the book, and even any controversial passages. As the survey guides the reader to noteworthy insights or passages in the book, the Bible student would then read those Bible passages and briefly study them. Popular survey books include Tremper Longman's *Introduction to Old Testament*, D.A. Carson's *Introduction to the New Testament*, and *The MacArthur Bible Handbook*. With that said, like the devotional method, the survey method is best used as a supplement to one's regular study, as it depends heavily on secondary resources rather than Scripture itself.

Conclusion

Each method has its benefits and weaknesses. Using each method in different seasons will help a person develop a fuller understanding of Scripture. We need to understand both the breadth and depth of Scripture—the forest and the trees. The more we know Scripture, the more God can use us for his kingdom (2 Tim 3:16-17). What are the various methods?

1. **The Read the Entire Bible Method**: It focuses on seeing the Bible's big picture by reading the entire Bible over a period of a few months, a year, or longer.
2. **The Expositional Method**: It focuses on studying a single book deeply.
3. **The Topical Method**: It focuses on understanding what the Bible says about a single topic like prayer, discipleship, or parenting.
4. **The Biographical Method**: It focuses on studying a single Bible character to learn from his or her traits and experiences.
5. **The Bible Memory Method**: It focuses on continually memorizing Scripture for encouragement and to conquer temptation.
6. **The Bible Mapping Method**: It focuses on reading a Bible book over and over again and outlining the chapters to develop a mind map of that book—functionally making one's mind a concordance.
7. **The Devotional Method**: It focuses on reading a devotional book to gain insight and encouragement.
8. **The Bible Survey Method**: It focuses on studying a Bible survey book to understand generally what happens in each

Bible book, including introductory material and major themes.

Reflection

1. In the reading, what method stood out most to you and why?
2. What do you typically do for Bible study? Is there a favorite study method that you use?
3. Which method do you most want to try and why?
4. What do you typically do to break out of periods of dryness in your Bible study?
5. What other questions or applications do you have from the reading?

Study Group Tips

Leading a small group using the Bible Teacher's Guide can be done in various ways. One format for leading a small group is the "study group" model, where each member prepares and shares in the teaching. This appendix will cover tips for facilitating a weekly study group.

1. Each week the members of the study group will read through a select chapter of the guide, answer the reflection questions (see Appendix 2), and come prepared to share in the group.

2. Prior to each meeting, a different member can be selected to lead the group and share Question 1 of the reflection questions, which is to give a short summary of the chapter read. This section of the gathering could last from five to fifteen minutes. This way, each member can develop their gift of teaching. It also will make them study harder during the week. Or, each week the same person could share the summary.

3. After the summary has been given, the leader for that week will facilitate discussions through the rest of the reflection questions and also ask select review questions from the chapter.

4. After discussion, the group will share prayer requests and pray for one another.

126

The strength of the study group is the fact that the members will be required to prepare their responses before the meeting, which will allow for easier discussion. In addition, each member will be given the opportunity to teach, which will further equip their ministry skills. The study group model has distinct advantages.

Reflection Questions

Writing is one of the best ways to learn. In class, we take notes and write papers, and these methods are used to help us learn and retain the material. The same is true with the Word of God. Obviously, all the authors of Scripture were writers. This helped them better learn the Scriptures and also enabled them to more effectively teach it. As you reflect on God's Word, using the Bible Teacher's Guide, take time to write so you can similarly grow both in your learning and teaching.

1. How would you summarize the main points of the text/chapter? Write a brief summary.

2. What stood out to you most in the reading? Did any of the contents trigger any memories or experiences? If so, please share them.

3. What follow–up questions did you have about the reading? What parts did you not fully agree with?

4. What applications did you take from the reading, and how do you plan to implement them into your life?

5. Write several commitment statements: As a result of my time studying God's Word, I will . . .

6. What are some practical ways to pray as a result of studying the text? Spend some time ministering to the Lord through prayer.

Walking the Romans Road

How can a person be saved? From what is he saved? How can someone have eternal life? Scripture teaches that after death each person will spend eternity either in heaven or hell. How can a person go to heaven?

Paul said this to Timothy:

> You, however, must continue in the things you have learned and are confident about. You know who taught you and how from infancy you have known the holy writings, which are able to give you wisdom for salvation through faith in Christ Jesus.
> 2 Timothy 3:14-15

One of the reasons God gave us Scripture is to make us wise for salvation. This means that without it, nobody can know how to be saved.

Well then, how can a people be saved and what are they being saved from? A common method of sharing the good news of salvation is through the Romans Road. One of the great themes, not only of the Bible, but specifically of the book of Romans is salvation. In Romans, the author, Paul, clearly details the steps we must take in order to be saved.

How can we be saved? What steps must we take?

Step One: We Must Accept that We Are Sinners

Romans 3:23 says, "For all have sinned and fall short of the glory of God." What does it mean to sin? The word sin means "to miss the mark." The mark we missed is reflecting God's image. When God created mankind in the Genesis narrative, he created man in the "image of God" (1:27). The "image of God" means many things, but probably, most importantly it means we were made to be holy just as he is holy. Man was made moral. We were meant to reflect God's holiness in every way: the way we think, the way we talk, and the way we act. And any time we miss the mark in these areas, we commit sin.

Furthermore, we do not only sin when we commit a sinful act such as lying, stealing, or cheating. Again, we sin anytime we have a wrong heart motive. The greatest commandments in Scripture are to "Love the Lord your God with all your heart and to love your neighbor as yourself" (Matt 22:36-40, paraphrase). Whenever we don't love God supremely and love others as ourselves, we sin and fall short of the glory of God. For this reason, man is always in a state of sinning. Sadly, even if our actions are good, our heart is bad. I have never loved God with my whole heart, mind, and soul, and neither has anybody else. Therefore, we have all sinned and fall short of the glory of God (Rom 3:23). We have all missed the mark of God's holiness and we must accept this.

What's the next step?

Step Two: We Must Understand We Are Under the Judgment of God

Why are we under the judgment of God? It is because of our sins. Scripture teaches that God is not only a loving God, but he is also a just God. And his justice requires judgment for each of our sins. Romans 6:23 says, "For the payoff of sin is death."

A payoff or wage is something we earn. Every time we sin, we earn the wage of death. What is death? Death really means separation. In physical death, the body is separated from the spirit, but in spiritual death, man is separated from God. Man currently lives in a state of spiritual death (cf. Eph 2:1-3). We do not love God, obey him, or know him as we should. Therefore, man is in a state of death.

Moreover, one day at our physical death, if we have not been saved, we will spend eternity separated from God in a very real hell. In hell, we will pay the wage for each of our sins. Therefore, in hell people will experience various degrees of punishment (cf. Lk 12:47-48). This places man in a very dangerous predicament—unholy and therefore under the judgment of God.

How should we respond to this? This leads us to our third step.

Step Three: We Must Recognize God Has Invited All to Accept His Free Gift of Salvation

Romans 6:23 does not stop at the wages of sin being death. It says, "For the payoff of sin is death, but the gift of God is eternal life in Christ Jesus our Lord." Because God loved everybody on the earth, he offered the free gift of eternal life, which anyone can receive through Jesus Christ.

Because it is a gift, it cannot be earned. We cannot work for it. Ephesians 2:8-9 says, "For by grace you are saved through faith, and this is not from yourselves, it is the gift of God; it is not from works, so that no one can boast."

Going to church, being baptized, giving to the poor, or doing any other righteous work does not save. Salvation is a gift that must be received from God. It is a gift that has been prepared by his effort alone.

How do we receive this free gift?

Step Four: We Must Believe Jesus Christ Died for Our Sins and Rose from the Dead

If we are going to receive this free gift, we must believe in God's Son, Jesus Christ. Because God loved us, cared for us, and didn't want us to be separated from him eternally, he sent his Son to die for our sins. Romans 5:8 says, "But God demonstrates his own love for us, in that while we were still sinners, Christ died for us." Similarly, John 3:16 says, "For this is the way God loved the world: He gave his one and only Son, so that everyone who believes in him will not perish but have eternal life." God so loved us that he gave his only Son for our sins.

Jesus Christ was a real, historical person who lived 2,000 years ago. He was born of a virgin. He lived a perfect life. He was put to death by the Romans and the Jews. And after he was buried, he rose again on the third day. In his death, he took our sins and God's wrath for them and gave us his perfect righteousness so we could be accepted by God. Second Corinthians 5:21 says, "God made the one who did not know sin to be sin for us, so that in him we would become the righteousness of God." God did all this so we could be saved from his wrath.

Christ's death satisfied the just anger of God over our sins. When God looked at Jesus on the cross, he saw us and our sins and therefore judged Jesus. And now, when God sees those who are saved, he sees his righteous Son and accepts us. In salvation, we have become the righteousness of God.

If we are going to be saved, if we are going to receive this free gift of salvation, we must believe in Christ's death, burial, and resurrection for our sins (cf. 1 Cor 15:3-5, Rom 10:9-10). Do you believe?

Step Five: We Must Confess Christ as Lord of Our Lives

Romans 10:9-10 says,

> Because if you confess with your mouth that Jesus is Lord and believe in your heart that God raised him from the dead, you will be saved. For with the heart one believes and thus has righteousness and with the mouth one confesses and thus has salvation.

Not only must we believe, but we must confess Christ as Lord of our lives. It is one thing to believe in Christ but another to follow Christ. Simple belief does not save. Christ must be our Lord. James said this: "...Even the demons believe that – and tremble with fear" (James 2:19), but the demons are not saved—Christ is not their Lord.

Another aspect of making Christ Lord is repentance. Repentance really means a change of mind that leads to a change of direction. Before we met Christ, we were living our own life and following our own sinful desires. But when we get saved, our mind and direction change. We start to follow Christ as Lord.

How do we make this commitment to the lordship of Christ so we can be saved? Paul said we must confess with our mouth "Jesus is Lord" as we believe in him. Romans 10:13 says, "For everyone who calls on the name of the Lord will be saved."

If you admit that you are a sinner and understand you are under God's wrath because of it; if you believe Jesus Christ is the Son of God, that he died on the cross for your sins, and rose from the dead for your salvation; if you are ready to turn from your sin and cling to Christ as Lord, you can be saved.

If this is your heart, then you can pray this prayer and commit to following Christ as your Lord.

> *Dear heavenly Father, I confess I am a sinner and have fallen short of your glory, what you made me for. I believe*

Jesus Christ died on the cross to pay the penalty for my sins and rose from the dead so I can have eternal life. I am turning away from my sin and accepting you as my Lord and Savior. Come into my life and change me. Thank you for your gift of salvation.

Scripture teaches that if you truly accepted Christ as your Lord, then you are a new creation. Second Corinthians 5:17 says, "So then, if anyone is in Christ, he is a new creation; what is old has passed away – look, what is new has come!" God has forgiven your sins (1 John 1:9), he has given you his Holy Spirit (Rom 8:15), and he is going to disciple you and make you into the image of his Son (cf. Rom 8:29). He will never leave you nor forsake you (Heb 13:5), and he will complete the work he has begun in your life (Phil 1:6). In heaven, angels and saints are rejoicing because of your commitment to Christ (Lk 15:7).

Praise God for his great salvation! May God keep you in his hand, empower you through the Holy Spirit, train you through mature believers, and use you to build his kingdom! "He who calls you is trustworthy, and he will in fact do this" (1 Thess 5:24). God bless you!

Coming Soon

Praise the Lord for your interest in studying and teaching God's Word. If God has blessed you through the BTG series, please partner with us in petitioning God to greatly use this series to encourage and build his Church. Also, please consider leaving an **Amazon review** and signing up for free book promotions. By doing this, you help spread the "Word." Thanks for your partnership in the gospel from the first day until now (Phil 1:4-5).

About the Author

Greg Brown earned his MA in religion and MA in teaching from Trinity International University, an MRE from Liberty University, and a PhD in theology from Louisiana Baptist University. He has served over sixteen years in pastoral ministry and currently serves as chaplain and professor at Handong Global University, teaching pastor at Handong International Congregation, and as a Navy Reserve chaplain.

Greg married his lovely wife, Tara Jayne, in 2006, and they have one daughter, Saiyah Grace. He enjoys going on dates with his wife, playing with his daughter, reading, writing, studying in coffee shops, working out, and following the NBA and UFC. His pursuit in life, simply stated, is "to know God and to be found faithful by Him."

To connect with Greg, please follow at http://www.pgregbrown.com.

Notes

[i] West, Robert M. How to Study the Bible (Value Books). Barbour Publishing, Inc. Kindle Edition.

[ii] Accessed 9/26/2019 https://bible.org/seriespage/13-facing-winter-seasons-2-timothy-49-22

[iii] Accessed 9/3/2019 from https://carm.org/mormonism/baptism-for-the-dead-in-1-corinthians-15-29

[iv] MacDonald, W. (1995). Believer's Bible Commentary: Old and New Testaments. (A. Farstad, Ed.) (p. 1957). Nashville: Thomas Nelson.

Made in the USA
Las Vegas, NV
30 March 2021